Let love be your guide!

Ruth Truman

How to Be
a Liberated Christian

How to Be
a Liberated Christian

Ruth Truman

ABINGDON

Nashville

How to Be a Liberated Christian

Copyright © 1981 by Abingdon

Library of Congress Cataloging in Publication Data

Truman, Ruth, 1931—
　How to be a liberated Christian.

　Bibliography: p.
　1. Christian life--1960–　.I. Title.
　BV4501.2.T77　　248.4　　80-27302

ISBN 0-687-17710-3

MANUFACTURED BY THE PARTHENON PRESS AT
NASHVILLE, TENNESSEE, UNITED STATES OF AMERICA

Dedicated to the people of the
Westlake United Methodist Church
who helped give birth to this book
and
to Melissa,
who asked the question:
How can I be a better Christian?

CONTENTS

FOREWORD

Liberation is a basic Christian doctrine long obscured by the mixture of tradition and cultural overlay. To the person trying to live as a Christian today, it is an essential doctrine.

It is hard to be a Christian in our time. Hard to know what to say, how to act, who to *be*. The world shouts so many words and points so many directions. In Christ and his teachings there are answers right for this liberated age and right for each of us.

Still, this is an exciting time to be alive. We are caught up in a tumult of change which carries us into an uncertain future. But such a future! Filled with intergalactic travel, discoveries of new forms of energy, explorations into the hidden minds of humans, and so much more. Yet change is frightening in that there is nothing sure, nothing that provides both the impetus and the security to move forward into the unknown.

Christ is the key—to the present and to the future. For even if the events of the world remained the same, we would change simply because the days passed and we grew older and more aware. We need a Key for each new day. Using his teachings we can unlock the secrets of living, as he would say, abundantly.

So in Christ I offer these words in the hope that they will help all of us become the best combination of liberation and Christianity: *liberated Christians!*

To help you in the search for your unique faith I have included suggestions for further reading at the end of each chapter. The titles contain a diversity of thought about living the Christian life. It is up to you to find the truth *right for you* in each of them.

I am indebted to Mark H. Wilmot, graduate student in the Fuller School of Clinical Psychology, Pasadena, CA, for assistance in researching these books, and to my father and mother, Rex and Allene Dixon, who have always prayed for me.

CHAPTER ONE

BECOMING A CHRISTIAN

When I was a little girl of nine I knelt at a church altar and asked Christ to come into my life. There were no loud bells ringing in my head, nor were there any dramatic visions. No one prayed prayers for me or implored God to save my soul. In fact no one but my father noticed me at all kneeling way down at the end of the altar rail. After all I was just a little girl.

About four years later at another altar came another special prayer for God to take my life and use it the way God wanted to. By now my body had grown to look more adult, and it seemed my prayer was more important to the people around me. This time they prayed with me. I felt a very close sense of God speaking within me. The presence of God, however, came not because of the people—they gave me support and encouragement—but because my spirit and the almighty Spirit were conversing.

In college God was again present when I had to surrender the love of a man in order to have peace inside. At thirty-five I fell on my knees asking God to come into my life anew, and God came. Today I still struggle to keep always new the commitment that began when I was nine. God recognized then what no one else did: that a spirit laid before Christ is ageless. It did not matter that my body was young, that I was not an adult, that my gender was female, or that my

11

name was Ruth. All that mattered was that I asked Christ to
come into my life and he did.

And that is how being a Christian begins: *somehow, some
way, you decide that more than anything else you want to be a
Christian and you invite Christ into your life. And he comes.*

No one needs to tell you *how* to become a Christian
beyond that simple act. You do not need to follow certain
steps that someone has devised. It is not necessary to have
water poured on your head or any other form of baptism.
You do not need to learn a catechism or memorize certain
passages of scripture. There are reasons that these forms
have been devised by churches and individuals, and
sometimes they are helpful, but all you really need to do is
to invite Christ into your life and then determine to live
and learn his way.

Searching for Christ in Churches

If you want to begin living the Christian life, let me
suggest that you start by looking in a *yes* church.

In any religion that goes back almost two thousand years
there are bound to be many offshoots of thought and
practice, and Christianity is no exception. You can find the
complete emotional spectrum in churches, from shouting
and dancing in the aisles to solemn worship services where
everything is preplanned and no variations are allowed.
You can find people and leaders who are so fanatic that all of
life is prescribed: how you should pray, what you should
think, how your marriage should be conducted, and so on. At
the other extreme will be people who attend church and
never mention it outside the sanctuary doors.

What I call a *yes* church has some special characteristics
that separate it from the extremes. Among them are the
following:

—you are encouraged to think out your faith;

—scripture is studied in its context and times;

—Christ is presented positively as the encourager of fullness of life;

—you are presented a positive image of yourself as a child of God; and

—you are constantly encouraged to grow both as a Christian and as an individual through opportunities to realize and use your God-given talents and abilities.

These may seem like qualities that should be common to all churches; yet in my forty-nine years of church-going (I started at four weeks) I have come to believe they are unique to churches which liberate the individual Christian. Let's take a closer look.

A church which encourages you to think will present more than one way of interpreting scripture. It will not prescribe how you should live, but will rather help you to develop a set of beliefs uniquely your own to guide your living. This is not to say that it will have no concepts of scriptural interpretation or guidelines for Christian living, but rather that it will expect you to think about, discuss, and examine its teachings, *and will accept you as a Christian even if you disagree.* This church will want you to bring your complete mental abilities to the consideration of scripture and will be comfortable if you challenge its thought. It will expect you to approach life in the same way. In short, if you are in a church which tells you what you *must* believe to be a Christian, if that church's way is the only way to get to heaven and all who do not follow it are doomed, you are not in a *yes* church.

Supporting the first characteristic but separate from it is the second: a *yes* church dares you to study scripture in its context and times. It has been said that you can prove anything by using (or abusing) the Bible, but to do so you must use the selective scripture approach: you simply select the scripture passages which support what you want to prove. For example, there is a small sect of Christianity that handles poisonous snakes to demonstrate faith, and they use Mark 16:17-18 to support their activities. A less extreme but more insidious illustration is the twisting of Paul's teaching on mutual submission of all Christians to one another in order to prove that women are ruled by and must remain submissive to men. (More about this later.)

In both of these illustrations scripture has been lifted out of its context and time. It is transplanted into this age without an understanding of the people to whom the scripture was written and the events then occurring which provoked the writing. Even more dangerous, scripture is not only literally translated but *literally applied,* as if no differences exist between the first and the twentieth centuries. A church that says *yes* to an abundant Christian life will be careful to teach scripture in its totality and will help you to understand its historical framework.

The Christ presented by a *yes* church will have a positive image—the third characteristic. Christ was a reformer in his day, not an effeminate, weak teacher. He preached a message so threatening to the religious establishment that they maneuvered his death. He made the individual important. He gave women a place of value equal to men. He crossed the barriers of race and religion. He condemned sacrilege in the temple and in its place encouraged sacrifice of the spirit.

By breaking traditional barriers Jesus set a new order of relationships between God, humankind, and individual persons. He established love as the factor defining his followers: love for God, love for others, and love for self. He envisioned love as the power to unleash the downtrodden, encourage the suffering, cleanse the sinner, and develop the saint.

So when you're looking for a *yes* church, the third

consideration is to listen closely to what they say about Christ. If he is your condemner, if his chief function is to initiate guilt within you, if his prime purpose is to return to judge mankind, you are not in a *yes* church. Christ does convict us of our sins through his teachings, and we *are* apt to experience guilt for our shortcomings and misdoings, but the positive church will point to the forgiving love and amazing grace of God in Christ. Christ will become your leader into ever-expanding avenues of life, giving you not only a positive image of God but also a positive image of yourself as a child of the Almighty.

A child of God is loved and cared for by the Father of whom Christ spoke. This child is cherished, is so important that the Father sent his son Jesus to teach and to lead all of us into "salvation." A church that emphasizes the positive elements of Christianity will teach a many-faceted salvation whose ultimate conclusion is the acceptance of self and of others. For example, salvation can mean that we are forgiven by God for all the wrong things we have ever thought or done. Obviously that takes a load off our backs and makes us feel better about ourselves. But salvation is more. Christ saves us *from* ourselves if we let him, from our characteristics and/or habits that make us unhappy with ourselves. But to be saved from something is to be saved *to become* something else. The self becomes a part of God's self.

If we are filled with hate and we ask the God/Christ to forgive us for hating, we are asking to have a powerful negative emotion removed from our lives. If at the same time we determine to "love our enemies" or to "love your neighbor as yourself" as Christ taught, we have taken the first step toward the positive emotion of love and freedom from hate. We may even recognize the need to come to terms with loving our "self" so that in turn we are better able to love others.

The *yes* church will encourage such a salvation of love that produces a positive image of yourself, but it will

probably go further. This church will help you understand
that by being free of hate you free those around you as you
begin to practice loving them. You are then "saved" from
hurtful relationships because you bring Christ's love to
life's unkindness. As others experience your love they
respond to you in different patterns, so that slowly you build
new relationships that return love; and in loving and being
loved you begin to feel good about yourself, and you extend
this "salvation" to others.

The *yes* church will encourage and help you recognize
these changes and then take you one step further: it will
provide opportunities for you to develop your talents and
abilities regardless of your gender. This characteristic is of
supreme importance to a Christian woman. Churches have
always encouraged members to participate in organization,
administration, and ministry. Not all churches, however
encourage full participation of women at all and/or any level
of activity. Some reserve the priesthood or clergy roles only
for men. Others do not allow or at least do not encourage
women to serve in top administrative positions and
councils. Some blatantly confine women to home and
servant tasks.

Such churches not only present negative self-images to
women, but also put barriers between male and female
Christians. They justify their actions by arguing from the
teachings of Paul as he ministered to the people of the first
century. They forget that Christ accepted women and men
for what they really were: living spirits spun off by God and
housed in gendered bodies. The positive church will
recognize with Paul that we are all "one in Christ Jesus"
(Gal. 3:28), and will help us understand the contextual
reasons for male disciples and early church leaders. It will
open wide its doors—and its offices of leadership—to all who
would follow Christ. This church will thereby unite men and
women as co-workers, liberating both to use their talents as
Christians.

When you look for this characteristic in a church, you will want to pay more attention to its actions than its words. Pronouncements of acceptance of women are fine and to be desired, but are meaningful only if these resolves are carried into the life of a church. It is easy to *say* that men and women are equal in Christ and then to apply first-century polity that allows only men to have active roles in the administrative and clerical church life. So look for a changing church: one that is saying the right things and has begun to take the proper actions. Actualized equality in a church frees both men and women, for by sharing the work of Christ, the organizational load becomes lighter for both sexes, and the joyous task of caring for others can be more easily accomplished.

In summary, a *yes* church encourages you to think, studies scripture in context, presents a positive Christ and thereby encourages a positive *you,* and offers opportunity for full personal growth, regardless of gender. These characteristics will make it easier for you to investigate, find, and develop your potential as a liberated Christian.

Searching for Christ in Relationships

Another avenue for discovering the Christian life is through relationships. The place to begin is by choosing your friends rather than letting them choose you. Friendships usually develop because people frequent the same places. Therefore, if you are looking for friends who have made a commitment to follow Christ, you will need to go places where these Christians go.

And where is that?

Committed Christians go everywhere, even to some places that "respectable" people wouldn't think of being seen!

The biggest collection of Christians will, ideally, be in the church you have found. But to know them as friends will take some effort on your part, for church services and perhaps coffee fellowships following worship will help you make acquaintances. Friendships come from studying together in small groups, working on committees, rubbing elbows on work projects, or chaperoning youth activities. In other words, to find Christian friends in the church may require your initiative to become a part of its activities.

Committed Christians will also be found at work, in the PTA, the League of Women Voters, the Rotary Club, or a myriad of other community organizations—or in the neighbor's house next door. The question is: How do you find them? How do you know?

One way is to watch the lives of people around you. Remember, it is not economic status, culture, intellect, or leadership that you are looking for. Rather it is *attitude*, the driving force in people's actions. Find love in a person and you may have found a Christian; add acceptance of people in every condition, secure trusting confidence in life, and joy that gives an inner strength even in crisis, and your search is usually over.

Now for the hard part. After the observing comes the initiating of friendship: a luncheon date, an invitation for coffee, or a singling out at a meeting so you can talk on a deeper level than the patter that brushes the surface of our lives. In order to discover their motivation you need to ask if Christ is, in fact, the meaningful difference you have observed. Then you will want to share that you are searching for Christianity and ask their help in your search.

Perhaps you're looking for an activist-type Christian friend who really attacks social issues. In that case you have to look literally everywhere. These Christians may be found working or volunteering in free clinics, emergency phone services, at inner-city rescue houses, shelters for drug addicts or ex-convicts, or on the city council fighting for a clean environment. They are involved in causes because they believe that the teaching of Jesus Christ leads us to join what we believe to the work that we do. They are literally trying to be God's hands to help create a better world.

As in other relationships, you will want to observe these people in action, perhaps work with them, to find out why they are involved, what *motivates* them. People are active in social causes for a myriad of reasons, but you are looking for the uniqueness Christ give to his followers. When you find a Christian activist, you have actually found someone who witnesses to his or her faith by demonstrating Christ's love to a suffering world.

Along this path you will probably make a lot of good friends who may or may not be Christians who will nevertheless enrich your life. Let them. Welcome new people, for they will help you grow. But in your search for the *Christian* relationship, keep looking until you find that special person.

Searching for Christ Through Scripture and Self Examination

Searching for Christ by seeking out a positive church and by developing relationships with Christians will inevitably lead you into a comparison of their lives and your own. Christ came teaching that people—you and I—could be made into new creations by believing in him. He talked of freeing the human spirit (John 8:32), of living a life of love that encompassed even one's enemies (Matt. 5:44). In the New Testament we are given not only his teachings but also glimpses into the lives of those who followed him.

For example, we see him releasing seven "demons" from the life of Mary of Magdala so that she became a devout follower who was entrusted with the news of the risen

Christ (Luke 8:2; Matt. 28:7). She loved Jesus so much that she came to the tomb to embalm his body, to serve him even in death.

Or we can look at the life of Peter, an unlearned fisherman. Peter took an initial step to follow Jesus, but gradually this rough, cursing man became convinced that Jesus was the Christ, the Messiah, the "Son of the living God." (Matt. 16:16). It was Peter who later preached to thousands, who opened the teachings of Christ to Gentiles as well as Jews, and who finally was crucified upside down for what he believed (Interpreter's Dictionary of the Bible, 3: 755. Nashville: (Abingdon Press, 1962).

The New Testament is filled with vignettes of people who were changed into new creations after meeting Christ. It was as though they saw mirrored in his spirit an image of what they could become; and as they walked with him, their lives gradually changed to fit the image.

And what about the people you meet today who are Christians—Christ ones? Begin to ask what it is in their lives that makes them different from others, what they have that may somehow be lacking in you. When they point you to Christ and his message of love and forgiveness, when you read his words and examine his actions, you may wonder if Christ can change you. You may see attitudes in yourself you no longer like—unkindness, greed, hatred, bigotry— attitudes that cannot share life space with love and acceptance of all humans as children of God.

These are the "sins" Christ came to save us from, sins that separate us from possessing the fullness of God's love. As you go through a process of self-examination, comparing your present self to the person you might become through following Christ's teachings, you gradually are made aware that it is, in fact, our *self* which Christ will save us from. Our fears, our inhibitions, our insecurities, our distrust of others. In short, all those things that bind us, that prevent us from realizing our full potential. It is these "burdens" which Christ offers to remove from our lives so that we may be liberated persons.

When you see what burdens you need to be free of, Christ stands ready to take them away. But to begin the Christian life does not require that you recognize all the "sins" of your self. If that were the case none of us would ever qualify! So let's analyze what beginning requires.

Starting the Christian Life

To begin is simply to commit your self—with all your strengths and weaknesses—to the forgiving, accepting love of Christ. It is to *decide* and hence to believe, that Christ really does accept you as you are, that he forgives your inadequacies and past actions, and in that forgiveness tells you to "go and sin no more" (John 8:11).

When you search for Christ in churches, relationships, and scripture, you will have as many ways of beginning suggested to you as the number of people you talk to. Some will say you must be "born again"; others will want you to be baptized; some will ask you to join the church; someone else will give you a card with four steps to follow. Perhaps you will pray a prayer that expresses your desire to follow him. Or maybe you will type your decision on a card and mount it on the dashboard of your car so you see it every time you travel. Or you may stand before a congregation and take the vows of church membership as evidence of your decision. But *the liberated Christian follows Christ in the style that is best and most fulfilling for him or her. The style of the commitment is not important, only that commitment occurs.*

Choosing to walk in Christ's way is the first part of commitment. It is the part *you* do. The second part is what God does through the powerful message of Christ. When you are ready to say, "Lord, here is my life," God is ready to accept you. If you have come to terms with this decision in emotional stress and tears, then you are likely to feel a sense of relief, of peace, and/or great joy. But great emotion is not necessary to know that God has forgiven and accepted you. Perhaps you simply decide, "Yes, I'm going to follow Christ from this minute on." And you do. With each passing day your strength in faith begins to grow so that one day you look back to that decision and realize just how momentous it was.

Christ is ready when you are. It is as simple as that. By making that commitment you have begun to live the Christian life. And you have also begun to pray. . . .

Suggested Additional Reading

Lewis, C. S. *The Best of C. S. Lewis*, "The Case for Christianity." New York: Macmillan, 1977.
Peale, Norman Vincent. *The Positive Power of Jesus Christ*. Wheaton, Ill.: Tyndale House, 1980.

CHAPTER TWO

LEARNING TO PRAY

What is prayer? To the casual observer it may appear to be words spoken into empty air, a cathartic exercise that generates its own peace. And for some it probably is.

But for most people prayer is infinitely more. It is a time for tuning in to universal power, for communing with the Spirit that lives within us: the Holy Spirit. Prayer is a means of unleashing a power or energy that affects the outcomes of problems, sicknesses, decisions.

To be realistic, one part of prayer *is* catharsis. Any time a person verbalizes those thoughts and feelings usually kept hidden, there is a therapeutic result. Even the most sensitive person, however, would cease to pray if his or her requests constantly disappeared into space, ineffectual and unanswered.

Pray-ers constantly state that their praying *does* effect both their inner and their outer world. It is not unusual to hear a person who has never believed in God or Christ exclaim over the action that occurred when they cried out to God and knew their prayer was answered. My experiences with people who have prayed bring me to these conclusions about prayer:

1. You don't have to believe in God for God to respond to your prayer.

2. Anybody can pray, at any age and in any language, and God will accept the prayer.
3. There are as many forms of prayer as there are pray-ers, though not all forms are equally effective.
4. Prayer is an indispensable activity for the maintenance of a whole personality.
5. Prayer is an action of the self that sets off a responsive action from the universal Self, or the undefinable power we call God.

Prayer and Belief

Refusing to pray or to admit that we do because we haven't decided whether God exists or not is a cop-out, a protective device mounted intellectually so that we won't have to get too involved in "religion." It is the supreme egotism of humankind that assumes we will someday know the answers to life origins and universal management, when in fact we cannot explain the functioning of the mind or the perfect formation of a baby's delicate ear. We stand in awe at the process of birth, comfortable with the miracle it is, but shake a stubborn fist at God for the equal miracle of death. It is not enough to assume there is no God and thereby wish away the unexplained power of orderly creation. It remains (thank God!) and so does the inevitable conclusion that a God-force is always present.

No one will ever give you an ultimate definition of God if you are a free-thinking individual. The only satisfactory definition must come from within you as you pray and study and mature in life and Christianity. So don't get hung up with trying to answer the God question. Instead try praying and let the answer come as it will.

What you *can* believe in is the power of the teachings of Christ. He was a soul who stood above us all, who challenged the lives of people of his day and of every generation since. His words seem so simple and forthright, yet they confound the wise. He joined with the universe to heal, to tie the past, present, and future together, and to demonstrate the incredible power and necessity of love for the flowering of the soul. He said that he and his Father were one (John 10:30); in other words, that his soul was a perfect operative replica of the God mystery. He also is described as "an advocate with the Father" (I John 2:1 KJV), a go-between for humans and God. Access is provided through the comprehension and practice of his message. To know him is to know the Unknown.

Prayer directed through Christ becomes a first step in the evolution of the soul, a growth process that completes the inner self by uniting it with the life-force we call God. Without prayer the soul potential withers.

But why Christ? Why not Buddha or Gandhi—or Moon, for that matter? This is an important question for the person deciding to be a Christian since it provides the first step in being a liberated Christian. *Liberation demands that we use our intelligence to sort out those truths that we personally can research and claim.*

Close analysis discloses that many great spiritual teachers have been given to humankind. Buddha and Gandhi were two of these, and the history books are filled with many more. Only the Christ, however, appears actually in focus with the universal God force. Such perfect attunement allowed him to perform "miracles"—to jump across limited human knowledge of universal laws to bring them into force in his day. Almost two thousand years later we are just beginning to discover in the scientific laboratory the power of the mind to reverse the sickness of the body, a power Christ used daily. Through a resurrection that the world has not been able to disprove or deny, we see the use of a power like creation itself—only in reverse. Instead of creating a physical body that we take for granted,

he created a spiritual body that was recognizable to human
eyes. No other teacher has demonstrated such God
qualities.

He did, however, join with *all* other spiritual teachers in
his use of prayer as the power connection with God. He told
us that the "kingdom of God is within" us (Luke 17:21). And
that the secret of his miracles—and our replication of
them—is tied to the mystery of prayer (John 14:12,13).

Christ also set himself apart from all teachers by saying
that "no one comes to the Father, but by me" (John 14:6
RSV). In other words God in his abundant mercy receives
all, but the channel or link between the unknown God and
the human soul is the seeable Jesus, the demonstration of
God. He is "the way, the truth, and the life" (John 14:6
KJV), in that when we follow his way we come to know
universal truths that open up our lives, lives that are
momentary opportunities for spiritual or Godlike evolution.

But these are only words *about* Christ. As persons who
start the Christian way—beginning with prayer—we have
a different perspective to complement our head knowledge.
We quickly begin to realize that *Christianity at its most
freeing is a combination of an understanding mind, a
God-tuned self, and a respected body.* For us the question
soon changes from "Why Christ?" to "Can there be any
other?"– and there cannot, for he is truly "God with us"
(Matt. 1:23).

How to Pray

So we begin to pray, if for no other reason than to see what
happens. I have already said that anybody can pray. Since
prayer is a discourse from the inner self it is not necessary to
be able to speak or hear or see, walk or move in order to pray.
And I am convinced that God hears the unverbalized cries of

the incompetent and incapable minds as well as the prayers of those who are fluent in ten languages, for we all share the exposure of our spirits before God. He hears and answers while we are yet speaking (Isa. 65:24) or when our spirits can only groan under the burden of physical life (Rom. 8:26).

But there are some ways to pray—and some old theologians' tales we may want to get rid of!

First, prayer does not require a prescribed format. Christ gave us an *example* in what we call "the Lord's Prayer" because his disciples were asking him how to pray (Matt. 6:9). In the example, he included a recognition of God and our puniness in contrast; a yearning for his presence with us on this physical plane; a request for our needs; an expressed awareness of our shortcomings toward ourselves, others, and God, and the need for forgiveness in those relationships; and a recognition of the glorious eternal power that preserves us all forever. What an example!

If you are a new pray-er, you may feel the way I do when faced with examples of physical exercises in a magazine: I'm so busy looking at the instructions that I finally give up on the exercises. So don't worry about the pattern yet. It will come in time, and when it does it will be uniquely yours.

Instead, try starting with this: prayer is conversation with the mysterious God-force. Conversation is made of (1) thinking and speaking, and (2) listening and understanding. The residue of conversation is (3) reflection. This pattern is simple because you already use it daily.

So begin to pray by verbalizing your thought to God. You may even begin with "God, if you're there. . . " Whether you express your thoughts aloud is your choice. Whisper if you want, or shout if you have need. The difference is for your benefit, not God's. From this beginning simply proceed to pour out your thoughts and feelings, joys and worries, as if Christ—your advocate with God—is right in front of you. Take the attitude that Christ is your confidant and counselor to whom you can tell all with perfect safety.

Envisioning the Christ with you is easier than trying to talk
to a nebulous, ill-defined God who has no human form.

The use of voice in such prayer does serve different
purposes for individuals. Speaking aloud helps some people
concentrate, but distracts others. At times the spoken
expression permits an emotional release not activated by
thought/internalized prayer. You will need to experiment to
find your pattern, but remember: the practiced ability to
pray in either silent or spoken manner allows you to build
an almost continuous communication stream with God, to
pray, as Paul enjoins us, "without ceasing" (I Thess. 5:17).

Prayer will take other forms when used in the Christian
community. For example, you may join a congregation in
reading prayers from a church bulletin or hymnal. Perhaps
the words don't say what you're feeling, and you wonder if
that makes them false, hollow. That depends on you.
Prayers read collectively in a service can have a synergystic
power for the household of faith, binding you with all the
others trying to follow Christ. Ancient rituals such as
communion services may seem cold and impersonal at first.
Eventually they become a part of you, *your* prayer, united
with all the men and women who have ever worshiped
Christ.

These group prayers are important for their inclusive-
ness. They tie believers together into the body of Christ. But
they cannot and must not take the place of your individual
prayers. They can be a blessing but *the* blessing of God in
your life comes from your individual interaction with the
Almighty.

So for the most part it is easy to do the thinking/talking
part of prayer. What trips up a lot of would-be pray-ers is the
other part—listening and understanding. Some people say
that they hear God speak "like a voice" in their heads.
Others will look askance at such declarations, yet admit to
following urges or directions to action that seem strangely
right. Still others witness to unusual circumstances

occurring that could only have been arranged by an outside force.

It is in the listening and understanding that we look for answers. Listening methods range from meditation to self-hypnosis imagery to simple quietness. I have used each of these—and one more: attempting to live every waking moment in a constant awareness of the God-presence. (Note: I said, "attempting," which does not mean succeeding!) Since quietness is the simplest, let's begin there.

After you have expressed your wants and needs, stay in your prayer attitude, but be quiet. Totally. Body, mind, telephone, and kids. In other words, for this kind of listening you need to designate some time alone. If your mind simply will not be quiet, then review slowly each request or prayer item. Holding it focused in your mind, ask God to speak, to direct you. Then listen to the inner voice. If after an adequate time you experience no directive thought, move on to the next concern. When you have completed such a prayer cycle you may have "heard" nothing. That's all right. You will soon begin to realize that your quiet time is making you a more peaceful individual, that answers to problems begin to appear when needed, and that you have a new confidence in your daily actions. When you get tuned in to God-power these things naturally happen.

Meditation is another listening format very popular today—and very spiritual. The techniques are many and well-marketed. However here is a simple meditative recipe: Locate yourself in a quiet, undisturbed place. Select a scripture verse or part of one. Either close your eyes to shut out interfering stimuli or focus them on a single item such as a picture or candle. Then force your mind to focus only on the scripture verse—for instance, "God so loved the world that he gave his only Son" (John 3:16 RSV). Let your mind flow with the meaning of each important word and freely associate between that word to your life and your world. Stay with it as long as you can, welcoming any bursts of

imagery that come. For example the word "God" may
engender a mental picture of a star-filled sky or a sun-
drenched beach. Put your self in the picture and become one
with it. Maybe your image will be powerful light: then
become one with the light and carry the image with you to
the next major words, "so loved," letting the light become
warm and all-enveloping. Continue until you have finished
the scripture and then quietly reflect over your meditation
experience.

Another approach to meditation is to use a phrase or
sound to push all other thoughts out of your mind and then
to hold your mind in emptiness. This practice of perfect
quiet gives the mind a total rest and renews it. We are
accustomed to resting other parts of our body, but we seldom
think of our mind as needing rest (except when we use
tranquilizers from the drugstore!). If you can train your
mind to concentrate you can also discipline it to emptiness.
Like all training, it takes practice. Each time a thought
emerges it must be dismissed. The beauty of this meditative
form is that into the emptiness a unique thought or phrase is
sometimes dropped, unique because it seems to come from
outside yourself. Sometimes its power and/or clarity is an
overwhelming experience, and you feel that you have truly
"heard" the voice of God. At the very least, the experience
can be described as having received an external thought
force, unprovoked and usually unrelated to your natural
thought patterns.

Another prayer technique is what I call *prayer imagery*.
This employs some of the mind control or self-hypnosis steps
for reaching an inner level of consciousness and usually
requires an external training process. Where this prayer
method deviates from mind control techniques is that after
going through the usual color progressions to reach an
"alpha" consciousness, the pray-er then invites Christ to be
the guide to the imagery experience. At its best, prayer
imagery gives the pray-er a strong sense of the presence of

Christ actively involved in the emotional, spiritual, and physical healing of those being prayed for. It also provides insights into events and decisions by applying the power of the Christ-force directly into the subconscious mind. This is a new prayer technique, but one that I believe will become a major force in individual lives as we approach the turn of the century.

All of these methods for "listening" to God work: simple quietness, meditation forms, prayer imagery. They do not all work equally for all people, and you must find what works for you.

There is, however, one more *form* of prayer that must not be left out in a Christian's repertoire of prayer opportunities: constant prayer. Praying without ceasing seems to be an impossible task for anyone but a monk. Since this directive about prayer bothered me, I decided to act on the suggestion to pray for everyone I met. At the time I was riding a bus to and from work, so I made a practice of studying the faces of people boarding the bus and then praying for them and the needs I thought their faces expressed. Two things happened: I developed a feeling of kinship with these strangers, and I learned the habit of praying constantly. The days became a running discourse with God, a constant openness to guidance in decisions, calls for strength, praise for beautiful moments. Even my old fears of being alone at night diminished as I could close a day of prayer with "OK, God, you take over," an acknowledgment that I didn't have to stay awake to protect my world. And now a further step has been added: to commit my sleep with its dreams and subconscious thought processes into the guiding presence of the Almighty.

So you see, prayer for a Christian may start as a conscious, unique act. But eventually it becomes a way of life and the source of direction and undergirding strength for that life. This is why I call it the cornerstone of Christian living. If you have no access to scripture, if you are cut off

from teaching and preaching, you can still commune with
God, still follow the example of Christ and "renew [your]
strength . . . mount up with wings as eagles" by turning to
your secret inner place for prayer (Isa. 40:31 KJV). In the
process you will experience a wholeness in your self, a
feeling of being completed because you are tied to the Source
of all our selves, and ultimately tied to all other humans
who share that "source" spirit. Recognition of the common-
ality of spirit in the God-source is Christian love begun.

Answers to Prayer

But what about prayer answers, you may ask? It's all well
and good to pray and listen, but what if I hear nothing and
what I ask for never comes? After all, Christ said, "Ask, and
it will be given you; seek, and you will find" (Matt. 7:7 RSV).
This sounds like a good system if it works. The question is,
will it? And if it doesn't, should I give up being a Christian?

The answers are yes, and no. The system does work, but
because many churches and people place a narrow
definition on the word "answer," people often feel their
prayers are ineffective. If we expect God to act at our
command (now God, I need you to do this, for example) we
may well be disappointed. As my husband says, God is not
our bellhop. Yet a lot of people pray this way.

Let's back up and take another look at Christ's directive.
In another place he seems to explain the "seek, and you will
find" when he says "seek first the kingdom of God, and his
righteousness, and all these things shall be added unto you"
(Matt. 6:33 KJV). He had just finished talking about daily
needs that are focused on maintaining the *body*. Christ
clarified "seeking prayer" by defining it as a spiritual
search, a search to become a part of the God-self. Such
prayer requests are always answered. When you seek to be a
part of God, God seeks to be a part of you.

On the other hand, Christ also says, "ask, and it will be given" in relation to talking about how the father will give gifts to his children. In our materialistic age some like to think that this means that if you pray for money you *should* get it, or protection of the body, or winning the game, or whatever. In short, if you're a Christian you should have one up on everybody else.

Well you do, but in the power of the spirit-self, not in the social milieu. For example, the Father's gifts that Christ promised us are most likely those described in Paul's letter to the Galatians as the fruits of the spirit: "love, joy, peace, longsuffering, gentleness, goodness, faith, meekness, temperance" (Gal. 5:22, 23 KJV). Certainly these attitude-changing gifts would make life far richer than mere money.

But Christ *did* promise to look after our needs. In discussing prayer he states that "your Father knows what you need before you ask him" (Matt. 6:8 RSV). We forget that needs and wants are not synonymous. Our needs are for food, clothing, and shelter, and even these can be reduced to a scarcity few Americans know about. Further, the supplying of these needs is often through the gifts of health, work capacity, and the mental ability to work out the details of finding and keeping a job.

So step one toward answered prayer is to ask for the right things: for spiritual strength, for wisdom to make right choices, for the gifts of the Spirit.

That's fine, you might say, as long as you have everything you need, but what about when you're desperate, your back is to the wall, and there's no way out? Doesn't God figure in it then, or do you just go on praying for love?

When I was a senior in college, I went home for Easter vacation knowing that there was more than forty dollars against my account beyond what I could earn. Unless it was paid I would not graduate. I had worked all through college, and my parents had also sacrificed and borrowed to educate my sister and me. No way could I ask them for more money. I had prayed a long time about my dilemma and finally committed it to God, realizing the Father knew my need. Arriving back from vacation I went to check my mail box, and in it was a small box addressed to me filled with pennies, nickles, dimes, and quarters. The total came within twenty-six cents of paying my debt to the college. The donor? Unknown.

More recently my husband's salary was hard put to cover college expenses, inflation, and a wedding. For seven months I had been regularly applying for work in my field, with no response. Our debt was mounting as I prayed about our money needs. Within a few weeks I signed a contract for a five-week job, earning just enough to pay the debt. Then I returned to my job search with the need cared for.

Such experiences convince me that prayer puts in force responses from the world around us that eventuate into answers. The mystery of those responses is a part of the God-mystery, some of which may be defined as scholars continue to explore the way the mind affects other minds. But defined or not, the response will still be couched in the creative will of God.

I am also convinced we should ask for only what we need. To ask for more from our limited universe may be to take someone else's share. If by virtue of birth, intelligence, and/or ability the Christian acquires more than he or she needs, much prayer and responsible consideration will need to be given to sharing extra wealth. For most of us, though, prayer is a matter of first seeking the gifts of the Spirit, and second, claiming the promise of Christ to supply our needs.

Step two in answered prayer is to learn to recognize the answers. Answers to requests for direction/guidance or to problems often come as "nudges" to take certain actions. These are valuable only if the pray-er follows through on them. God gives the idea, perhaps even prepares the circumstances, but we must still take the action. ("Faith without works is dead"—James 2:20, 26 KJV.) Acting on the nudges and trusting the action and outcome to God is one way to effect answers to prayer. Answers also come through intuitive flashes, dreams, other people's statements or deeds, or through the inner resolution of conflict.

Prayer answers are tied to the complexity of universal resources. Someone has a need. Perhaps he or she talks about it in a group. Later as they concentrate in prayer on the need, a member of the group feels the necessity to respond, and in so doing becomes part of the answer. The power of suggestion, mental telepathy, human response are a part of God's resources in this scenario. How else could I be praying in my bedroom for a driver to assist a group of touring Samoan Christians, have the telephone ring, and pick it up to hear "Ruth, God has really been working on me. I've got to drive a bus for you"? The problem solution came through tapping the universal Source.

Not all answers are so easy to see or so quick to occur. It is difficult to "wait on the Lord" (Ps. 27:14). We are creatures of body-life time, impatient because we measure time in minutes instead of aeons. Sometimes we must seem to God like children flailing arms and feet in a tantrum of protest over God's slowness and our limitations. Yet waiting will produce internal growth if we let it. Looking back, we often realize that if what we prayed for so intently had occurred when *we* wanted it to, we would not have been able to handle it. Our answer was deferred to God's timetable.

One thing should be obvious by now: prayer is a vehicle for providing spiritual and personal growth and direction, not a substitute for intelligence, logic, education, and effort. Prayer activates and frees the individual to greater use of his or her faculties. When the answer to a major problem is not obvious, we should shift to prayer for *daily* (or hourly) direction, for right decisions in working out a solution, for support for our continued efforts in applying what we know. It may also be the time to seek help from someone else: a

counselor, minister, resourceful friend. Sometimes our
prayer can't be answered because we are so subjectively
caught in our dilemma that God must use someone else to
show us the way out. In short, when we wait on God, we go
about our daily lives with a sense of heightened awareness
of possibilities. Or as my father would say, "Keep casting
your bread on the water till one piece turns up buttered."

There is, however, another way to handle the difference
between God's time and our time. When Christ spoke about
the Father already knowing what we need, he was also
teaching that we don't have to hammer on the door of
heaven to have our prayers heard and answered. *If we have
faith enough,* we can trust God to fulfill his will in our
lives—his way, not ours. Instead of praying frantically,
"Lord I've got to have this job," we can pray, "Lord, lead me
into thy will for my life and give me awareness and courage
to follow." This is a difficult prayer to pray. It means that we
claim God's promise to provide for us, to answer our prayers
in what ultimately is most meaningful for our lives. And
then we leave the request as a commitment to God and go on
with living, not worrying about the outcome. We do,
however, remain in constant contact with God, ready to take
those opportunities that are put in our paths.

*Commitment to the will of God is the third and most
complex aspect of prayer.* To hand over the design and
fulfillment of one's life to the complete direction of God is
utter insanity in our ambitious, achievement-oriented
world. Yet this is precisely what the disciples did when they
left their families and work to follow Jesus. Their act of
following meant leaving behind the plans to become
"Zebedee and Sons, Inc." for James and John (Mark 1:19), or
a wealthy and respected "Dr." Luke. Yet who would know
these men today if they had not followed? The rich young
ruler remains nameless in history, noted only for his
inability to give up his riches to follow Christ.

Surrendering one's life into the will of God is a step many

Christians are fearful or unable to take. Such an act does not mean divorcing one's self from reality, but rather allowing the totality of decision-making to be ruled by the teachings of Christ and the purposes of God, instead of by society.

As a beginning Christian you should know that someday you will be confronted with the overwhelming need either to surrender your life totally or to cut out. Each of us faces this battle between God and self at some point. Only you can decide the outcome. I can simply tell you that on the other side of surrender lies the total peace and security of knowing that nothing can ever destroy your spirit, for God is with you. Because God is, you are.

Learning to pray, then, is a lifetime project. It requires discipline and persistence. It also becomes a primary resource for coping with life. As we mature, so will the forms of prayer we use to address an ever-growing experience with God.

Thinking/speaking, listening/understanding, and reflection will become a way of life. Obvious prayer answers, so important in the beginning, will later blend into simple trust that the God who has led us this far will remain with us the rest of the way. Ultimately prayer becomes the transitional vehicle, the soul opener, that prepares and transports the spirit freed by death into deathless Universal Life.

Christ is the link between us and the unknown, all powerful God-force. He is the way to truth that yields abundant life. The key to that life is prayer.

Suggested Additional Reading

Eastman, Dick. *The Hour That Changes the World*. Grand Rapids: Baker Book House, 1978.

Keck, Robert. *The Spirit of Synergy: God's Power and You*. Nashville: Abingdon, 1978.

Wood, Robert. *A Thirty-Day Experiment in Prayer*. Nashville: The Upper Room, 1978.

CHAPTER THREE

LEARNING
TO READ

As prayer is the cornerstone of the Christian life, so the knowledge of the scriptures becomes the foundation for that life. And even as prayer forms need to be freed to fit each person's unique requirements, so does the approach to Bible reading and study need to be liberated.

The Bible is a book just like every other book you've ever read: many words printed on paper, words you understand. They are for the most part the same words used in textbooks at school, in business reports at work, in the books and papers we read all the time. Regular, ordinary words. It is only when the words are arranged into sentences and gathered together into these sixty-six "books" and letters that they are called "God's word."

God did not actually write the words. People did. People who lived in a prayerful attitude, people who wanted to preserve their history, people who could foresee the future, people who walked with Christ, and people who set the Christian church in motion.

None of these people knew they were writing "the Bible." They were individuals like you and me living out their lives. The difference is that they were chosen to receive and/or express some particular message to the people around them, a message so powerful that it was seen by their peers and later by church scholars as coming from God.

The meaning of what these writers said is not always

understood by readers of the Bible. For example, the Bible opens with the story of how the world began, its creation. But there are actually two creation stories (Gen. 1:1–2;4*a*; Gen. 2:4*b*-25), a fact that raises some questions. If this is the word of God, why are there two stories? Never mind the much bigger question of the validity of the stories themselves or what we know today from the scientific discoveries about the universe! Surely it can be assumed that the authentic word from God should have only one version of the creation. . . .

Let this be a warning to you. You are about to begin on a journey into a book of books that will keep unfolding for an entire lifetime if you will let it. Today's mystery will be tomorrow's discovery.

So let's get one thing straight: the Bible in its *book form* is not sacred. *Rather it is holy because of the eternal truths that are on its pages.* Something sacred is venerated, prayed to, worshiped. The Bible will be of little use to you if you treat it that way, although you will meet Christians who do. A sacred book would never be marked up, never have notes in its margin, never be carried in the glove compartment of the car. Yet a Bible used this way becomes a vital part of a Christian's life. Try treating the book like the history textbook that it is: the history of God at work in the life of people and nations.

Choosing a Bible

When you walk into the bookstore to buy your first Bible, be prepared: there may be a dozen versions for you to choose from. First, two creation stories, and now a dozen Bibles! It looks like in two thousand years Christianity could do a better job of getting its act together! But that is precisely the point. The array of Bibles to choose from is evidence of an increasing determination by Christians to provide people with the word of God in its most accurate and/or readable form.

The versions—which are more accurately called translations—generally fall into three categories, which I will call traditional, exact modern, and vernacular modern. They all contain at least the same sixty-six books and say essentially the same thing. Their differences lie in their historical roots or in the purpose of the translation. *No matter which one you choose to read, you will still be reading "the word of God."* However, to illustrate their differences and to help you in your choice, I will briefly describe each category and give examples of versions frequently used by Christians.

The traditional Bible of English-speaking Christianity is the King James Version, published in 1611 (New Testament in Four Versions, Christianity Today Edition, 1963). This is the version that most people recognize by its use of "thee" and "thou" instead of the modern pronoun "you." Since it was the translation in common use until the English Revised Version of 1881 and the American Revised Version of 1901, its language became for many people synonymous with the language of God. There are people who argue that tampering with the King James Version or using any other version is denial of the correct word of God.

However, the King James Version of the New Testament was based upon a Greek text marred by an accumulation of errors from fourteen centuries of manuscript copying. Further, over three hundred English words that were in common usage in 1600 have since come to have other meanings, such as "ghost" for "spirit" or "wealth" for "well-being." Later editions are based on better and earlier Greek manuscripts, and also use more current language.

Nevertheless, the King James Bible is a masterpiece of the English language and houses within its lyrical phrases much of the theology and phraseology of the Christian church. The words of ancient and current prayers written into church liturgy and uttered from pulpits give testimony to this influence.

In the second category, which I call exact modern, are numerous translations that were undertaken by groups of biblical scholars at the request of church bodies or councils. These include among others the Revised Standard Version, first published in 1946: The New English Bible, 1961, 1970; and The Jerusalem Bible, 1966. These versions are generally acknowledged to be the most accurate translations available today in the sense of linguistic scholarship, the use of earliest manuscripts, and the translation of meanings of words into modern English. They are easy to read because they follow our familiar paragraph structure of prose writing, and in the Jerusalem and New English versions the numbers for the familiar chapter and verse divisions of the King James Version are set in the margin where they do not interrupt the sentence flow. Further, each of these versions can be purchased in editions containing introductory and background material for each of the books and for the translation as a whole.

The Jerusalem Bible also contains additional books beyond the sixty-six—which are termed the "apocryphal" books. These are Old Testament books from the Greek Bible, the Septuagint, used during the centuries just before Christ—by the Jews of the Dispersion. This Bible is otherwise identical with the Hebrew Bible that was fixed by the early Christian church. These apocryphal books also make the difference between Roman Catholic and Protestant editions of scripture. They include I Esdras, Odes, and Psalms of Solomon. In addition The Jerusalem Bible contains books that are a part of the Christian canon, books regarded by parts of the church as being inspired in the same way as the books of the Hebrew Bible. Judith, Tobit, the Book of Wisdom (Wisdom of Solomon), Ecclesiasticus (Wisdom of Sirach), Baruch, and chapters 13 and 14 of Daniel comprise these writings. For the beginning reader, however, these books are not a part of the mainstream of scriptural inclusion and can be considered secondary for scriptural study.

The third group of Bible versions I have termed vernacular modern. This is not to say that they are lacking in scholarship or exactness, but rather that the intent of the translator is more obviously placed on readability by using vernacular and idiomatic language. In this group can be placed *Good News For Modern Man, The Way, (The Living Bible),* and J. B. Phillips' *New Testament in Modern English.* These are the versions you might want to keep in the car or by a favorite chair to read for enjoyment and inspiration. Or you might wish to start your reading with one of these to quickly familiarize yourself with its content. If you are buying a study Bible you will want a medium-sized print on a sturdy paper suitable for marking. It might also include a concordance or cross-reference system to help you find other sections dealing with similar subject matter. A four-translation edition will allow you to quickly compare differences in language for better understanding. Take time to compare the versions and then choose the Bible that fits you best, along with the print and paper easiest for you to use. On the other hand, a pocket-sized paperback may be right to carry in the car.

Whatever Bible you choose in the beginning will be just that—your first choice. As you begin to absorb its words you will soon find that you will want more than one version, and probably one from each category. The King James will provide soul-satisfying lyricism, the exact modern will give you the most careful biblical detail, and the vernacular modern will fill your empty hours.

Mapping a Reading Plan

So now you've got a Bible. The question is, what will you do with it? The Old Testament starts out pretty exciting, but somehow unbelievable. It's just such a *big* beginning! But if you start at the first New Testament book you could feel snowed under with genealogy (Matt. 1:1-16). If you decide to begin with Paul and tackle Romans you may drown in first-century theology. Obviously you have to have a plan.

Ask yourself, "What do I want to know first?" If your answer is "Who was Christ?" then read the Gospels first: Matthew, Mark, Luke, John. Each has a slightly different perspective and therefore a unique value to the beginning Christian. You do not need to read them in order. Rather select one and read it several times before moving to another. Let the words of Christ be your first focus; then read to discover his actions; then to center on his followers. From there you will be able to devise your own focus.

As with any textbook assignment, it is a good idea to read the whole book through once for content. On the second reading, use a marking pen and a notebook. Mark those words or passages which seem especially important to you; write down your thoughts and/or conclusions about what you have read. Don't feel you must read "a chapter a day" (as someone will surely tell you!) but instead set some maximum/minimum limitations *that fit your life*. The minimum need is obvious—to keep reading and to develop the daily habit. The maximum limitation is to help keep your life in balance: reading scripture all day keeps real life far away! Besides you need time to *think* about what you have read, which you can't do if you are still reading.

If your "what do I want to know?" answer is history, then tackle the first five books of the Old Testament (Genesis, Exodus, Leviticus, Numbers, and Deuteronomy). Here is the story of the development of the Jewish people, of God's work among them, their laws and ways. If it is Christian history you want, read Acts, in the New Testament, and glimpse the struggles of the early church to become truly the church. Follow this up with some of the Epistles—letters to the churches at Galatia, Ephesus, Thessalonica (Galatians, Ephesians, Thessalonians). Whichever way you begin, be sure you follow your orignal choices with reading in the other two areas before you branch out to other books. This way you will build a foundation that includes the Christ focus, the development of the early church, and the historical roots of Christianity.

After you have begun to read regularly you may feel the need of some outside source for clarification or assistance. Look first in your church for a study group or church-school class that will not only provide guidance but will stimulate your thinking by exposing you to other people's interpretations of scripture. This is the time for a concordance, a book designed to give you references using certain key words, so that you can quickly compare scripture passages. Some versions have concordances designed specifically for that translation, such as the *Concordance of the New English Bible—New Testament* (Grand Rapids: Zondervan Publishing House, 1964).

If you purchased a vernacular modern edition, this may be the time to buy a study Bible that includes a concordance. An excellent example of this combination in the King James Version is the *Thompson Chain Reference Bible* (Indianapolis: B. Kirkbride Bible Co.), which groups scriptures by topics, and provides cross-references for many words, maps of Bible times, and so on. *Whatever you choose at this point should be an outgrowth of your own personal study needs*, not a book that someone else tells you to use. Consider their judgment and recommendations, but also consider the person you are. If you rarely use a study aid, you may want to purchase a small paperback concordance instead of an expensive, expansive hardbound edition.

By now you may also have discovered devotional books, so called because of an earlier emphasis on setting aside a certain time each day for devotion to God. These are usually composed of scripture verses or topics, each one discussed in one or two paragraphs. Some include prayers and/or thoughts to center on during the day. They are frequently available through your church in quarterly editions and go by names like *The Upper Room* (United Methodist), *These Days* (Presbyterian), *Daily Blessing* (Nondenominational). There are also many books on the market designed for daily use. If these short readings are helpful to you, use them. However, *don't let them be the substitute for your own reading program!* It is easy to fool yourself into thinking you are reading sufficiently because you use a daily inspirational writing, when in fact you are not reading scripture at all.

Other Bible study helps fill entire catalogs. There are commentaries that give you theological and historical background, Bible dictionaries, Bible atlases, Bibles designed for young readers, and books focused on certain portions or single books of the Bible. The array can be overwhelming—and unnecessarily confusing. Ask your pastor or a Christian whose life-style you appreciate for their recommendations. But above all, keep your study simple. Too many books *about* the scripture can so consume your time that you find you are not reading the scripture itself. Choose carefully and expand slowly.

Another way to develop a reading plan is to use the lectionary scripture passages selected to follow the church year and to keep you reading with unfolding Christian worship. Prior to Easter you would be reading about the trial and crucifixion of Jesus, while at Christmas you would be directed to his birth story.

Developing your own reading plan allows you to begin where *your* interests are and read in a style and amount confortable for you. It frees you to choose among Bible versions and study helps, to select what you need. *It also puts the responsibility for reading squarely on you,* just as it was up to you to develop a prayer life and style. Without

prayer your faith withers, and without scriptural knowledge and understanding it cannot grow. For both of these
activities, however, there is a problem in today's busy life:
finding time.

A Time to Be

You won't be in a church or study group very long before
you hear someone say: "The problem is not the reading, or
the understanding. It's just that I never have the time." And
you may find yourself in complete agreement with the
speaker!

Finding time—for anything—means setting priorities.
What are the ten most important time-consumers in your
day? Job? Children? Commuting? Meal preparation?
Walking the dog? For the Christian who wants to grow in
faith, time for reading and/or studying the Bible has to have
a high priority.

There are ways to develop the time you are now losing
into productive Bible time. For example, you may be driving
several miles to work each day. The Bible is available on
cassette tapes, and you can listen to your chosen books as
you ride. A busy mother can use a child's nap time for
reading and contemplation. Keeping a Bible with you in
your purse, car, desk, or shirt pocket allows the use of
waiting times (i.e., gas lines, doctor's offices, appointments)
to keep you on your reading plan. And planning is the key,
for if you have not predetermined your use of this time, you
will probably end up reading a 1975 copy of Redbook or
fuming at the inconvenience of waiting. Analyze your day
and identify any such possibilities.

A better solution to finding time is to choose a specific
time when you are least likely to be interrupted. Some
people get up a half-hour earlier to begin their day with

Bible reading. Others reserve the last hour before sleeping. Some do both. The point is that *you* are really the one who decides what you do with your time. If you *want* to read the Bible you will. But developing the habit takes some discipline—or the help of a friend. . . .

Planning to read a certain part of scripture each day at the same time (but not place) as a friend or spouse can be a helpful technique. This gives you a sense of closeness to the person and enriches your relationship, particularly when it is followed by a sharing telephone call or letter. For example, a husband at work uses a mid-morning break to read, knowing that his wife at her job or home has also paused to read. Not only does the scripture speak to them, but their love surrounds them as well. The same technique can be used by a family separated by many miles, or by a study group in your community.

Many people combine time for meditative prayer with Bible study, using one to accent the other. The openness of the quiet mind heightens one's receptivity to the truths in the Bible.

Like prayer, Bible reading can be done anytime, anywhere. If portions of scripture are committed to memory, they can then be recalled and considered in the midst of a crowd. The words of Jesus are soon "with you always" and his presence becomes continually nearer (Matt. 28:20).

Commitment, prayer, and Bible reading are the guideposts for your Christian life. A liberated Christian determines his or her own patterns for each of these actions, and in so doing has already begun to develop a unique life-style. The development of the inner soul or self must now begin to be translated into external personality, for that translation is what other people refer to when they hear someone say, "I am a Christian." So get up off your knees, put your Bible away for the moment, and let's go live a little . . .

Suggested Additional Reading

Barclay, William. *The Gospel of John,* vol. I. Philadelphia: Westminster Press, 1979.

New International Version, *Light to Live By.* Grand Rapids: Zondervan, 1979.

Phillips, J. B. *For This Day.* Waco, Tex.: Word Books, 1976.

Smedes, Lewis B. *Love Within Limits.* Grand Rapids, Eerdmans, 1978.

CHAPTER FOUR

CHOOSING
A LIFE-STYLE

In the seventh chapter of John we have two important glimpses of the life-style choices Christ made in his society. First we see his brothers asking him to go to a festival in Jerusalem. He tells them that the "right" time hasn't come for him, but that *they* need not be concerned about going because "any time is right" for them (John 7:7). Later he goes to Jerusalem on his own "almost in secret" (John 7:10 NEB), and about halfway through the festival begins to teach in public. Clearly Christ was acting on his own inner-directed schedule.

While he is there he challenges the crowd about his sabbath-breaking activities— and theirs. He defends the healing he has done, which they consider working on the sabbath. He then points out that their custom of circumcising a new baby on the sabbath is also a violation of the day, albeit done to avoid breaking the law of Moses. In short their exception justifies his exception! Christ defends his life-style on the very basis that his accusers defend theirs; yet the activities are dissimilar.

The way we live—our life-style—never happens accidentally. It emerges from choices like the ones Christ made in this illustration, daily choices about *all* acts of life. For example, a person who *chooses* the easiest tasks, the least commitment to society, who rarely makes the effort to acquire or save anything beyond the day's needs, is soon

dubbed by society as a person content to "just get by";
another may work night and day and be termed a
"workaholic." The styles are made from choices.

A *Christian* life-style includes an added dimension—the
Christian has the responsibility of making choices that will
reflect his or her Christ-centered inner direction, the
direction received through prayer and scripture. Further,
the liberated Christian may find himself or herself in the
position of doing just what Christ did: finding the basis of
choices in a new and/or different interpretation of church
tradition and scriptural teaching.

In the first chapter I talked about finding a *yes* church, a
church that gives you a positive image of Christ and
yourself. You may have wondered why this is necessary.

In distinct opposition to the positive church are those
groups of Christians who appear to define the Christian life
by what a person does *not* do: Christians do not dance, do not
drink, do not gamble, do not use drugs. Perhaps they also do
not attend movies or theatrical performances, do not wear
jewelry (or buttons, for that matter!), do not show anger or
have a temper, etcetera. Such a negative approach to
life-style soon becomes overwhelming. Carried to its
ultimate conclusion an individual is allowed to eat
sparingly, work at specifically approved vocations, sleep,
read the Bible, and pray, all the while dressed in clothes
that cover everything but the extremities of the body.

The choice to abstain from any or all of these actions *may*
be part of a Christian's life, but such a negative definition of
Christianity becomes a prison to the personality when it is
dictated by a church or clergyman and reinforced by guilt or
fear of eternal damnation.

Christ said it so well when talking to the crowd about his
sabbath work: "Do not judge superficially, but be just in
your judgements" (John 7:24 NEB). In other words, Christ
was demanding that his accusers examine the reasoning for

his choice of action rather than making judgments out of their own reference format, i.e., custom.

The liberated Christian chooses to be free from such dictations of church and/or custom, free to make individual prayerful choices about daily life actions. Freedom always carries the price of responsibility. In some ways it is easier to have a dictated life-style, to do or not do specific things and thus automatically get into the kingdom of heaven. Freedom from this kind of dictation actually increases the responsibility of individual choices. Free responsibility is better, however, than having someone else's choices imposed on our relationship with Christ.

About now you maybe asking if there are some specific directions in the New Testament for how a Christian should live? And perhaps you are wondering if most of the dictates of churches are based on scripture.

Some are, and some aren't.

Some are a fusion of a scriptural interpretation and a particular influence on society. The "evil" of that time may be seen in retrospect as an "unknown" or "change" influence that was threatening the moral "status quo" and was denounced by combining fear and scripture. For example, the invention of moving-picture film, and going to the movies, which had to be shown in dark theaters increased the opportunities for familiarities between unchaperoned sexes while showing "immoral" behavior on the screen. Wholesale denouncement of "movies" was based on the fear of a change in moral patterns acceptable to that time, not on a scriptural injunction to stay away from movies.

Sometimes specific dictates have entered into Christians' life-styles through the influential preaching of one or two men, become identified with the "Christian" life, and then been defended by later generations simply because they were a part of the handed-down acceptable life-style package. From such life-style impositions have come the charges of hypocrisy from people outside the church who heard grand pronouncements of intended changes from new converts who later could not carry through on their intended life-styles. If the intentions of life-style choices had come from within the individual instead of being imposed from without, had evolved from study, prayer, and personal growth, and had developed as the individual matured, then those intentions would have been more apt to succeed.

The message of the scripture is that God looks upon the heart, i.e., the attitude behind the act. Where Christians are constrained by the legalities of churches today, so the early church was often bound by the legalism of the Jewish law. When he was challenged about not washing his hands before eating, Christ responded: "It is the thought-life that pollutes" (Mark 7:15 TLB). What comes from within is what condemns us—envy, jealousy, greed, deceit. It is up to us to make our own choices of daily actions that will demonstrate the fruits of the spirit of Christ within us.

Liberated Christians will deliberately make choices backed by worship, prayer, and study—choices that will speak their faith to the world around them. They will also give to other Christians the same privilege of choice, supporting them with a spirit of acceptance and understanding. They will recognize that just as God's "children" are at different levels of intelligence, age, race, and sex, so they will make different choices in their everyday enactment of faith. Differences of scriptural interpretation or church doctrine will not be allowed to separate liberated Christians from other people trying to follow Chirst. They will not draw a circle that includes themselves "in" and leaves everybody else in Christendom "out."

Guidelines for Life-style Development

Developing a Christian life-style will take a lifetime, so you can hardly expect to map one out in a couple of hours.

However, a few hours *can* produce some guidelines for beginning. These will have to be modified or entirely changed from time to time, mostly because *you* will change. Or your job. Or society. Or your spouse. Or your kids. In other words, expect to evolve because the Christian you are is first of all *you.*

Since becoming a Christian doesn't give you a new intellect, body, or basic personality, you will need to begin by understanding who you are. *The more you comprehend and therefore develop yourself, the more useful you will be in the demonstration of God in the world.* Someone has said we are God's hands and feet, in which case we ought to make sure they are well trained and thoroughly operative in our present society!

Your self is a mixture of attitudes, talents, trained abilities, and programmed expectations. In starting this part of your Christian life planning, remember that what you do now should be repeated at five-to ten-year intervals to accommodate for the changes time and circumstances will bring into your life.

Start by taking out a sheet of paper and putting down four headings across the top: Attitudes, Talents, Trained Abilities, Programmed Expectations,. List under *attitudes* those characteristics of your spirit/self that you recognize, e.g., (I am) kind, hot-tempered, jealous, loving. On a separate sheet, arrange your completed list from what you see as the most dominant attitude to the least. Then give your list to someone who knows you very well and whom you trust with this confidential report. Ask this person to evaluate and rearrange it to match the way he or she sees you. Listen to the responses. Try to be objective in viewing yourself from the inside and the outside. Then set the list aside and repeat this exercise with your *talents* (e.g., logic, nurturing, artistic ability); and again repeat it for your *trained abilities,* such as computer programming, nursery school teaching, composing.

EXAMPLE OF PERSONAL INVENTORY

Attitudes	Talents	Trained Abilities	Programmed Expectations
Eager to learn	Meeting people	Public Speaker	Mother: always achieve more
Critical	Thinking	Chair for meetings	Father: be moral—I am!
Authoritative	Music	Good driver	Husband/wife take care of
Excited about life	Making people	Researcher	him/her
Concerned about	feel at ease	Computer programmer	Children: always be there
others	Working with hands	Macramé craftsperson	Boss: produce on time with
Adventuresome	Logic		excellent product
Bored			Church School Class: never
			let them down (impossible!)
			Me: live a full life
			love people
			be faithful to my
			commitments
			try to be all things to
			all the people in my
			life! (can't do this; guilt
			comes from this)

CHRIST EXPECTATIONS

Attitudes
Listen more,
   dictate less
Live, not just
   think about it
Act out my concern

Talents
Sing in church
   choir
Be a greeter
Teach children
   how to use hands

*Trained
Abilities*
Volunteer to drive for
   convalescent home
Take world outreach
   committee

Expectations
Figure out what is most
   important for me as a Christian
   whether others like it or not
Quit trying to be all things
   to all these people and
   accept myself; be honest
   in my relationships with
   others
Try to find a balance between
   spouse's *needs* and wants;
   help him/her learn how to do
   things for self so he/she is
   not so dependent on me

The fourth category, programmed expectations, will be more difficult. From the day you were born people have been programming you. In school, at the movies, around the dinner table, people have been telling you how to act, what to say, what you should *think*, i.e., how to be. Now you must separate the things your mother, father, siblings, boss, fiancé, or spouse expects of you from the expectations, hopes, and dreams you have for yourself. You will probably be able to quickly sort out a few expectations under various people's names, but the crucial sorting must be done under your own name. Are the expectations for your life actually yours—or over time have they been absorbed from someone else? When this has been clarified to your satisfaction then prioritize these expectations. You will then have a list of life goals important to the person you currently are.

Up to this point nothing about your self-knowing search is any different from goal searches in most personal development books. It is the next list that makes the difference. In the category of expectations add the name Christ. Now look at your lists of attitudes, talents, and trained abilities. Look at your personal expectations. Ask yourself: In view of the person I am, what does Christ expect of me? How does he expect my priorities to change? Are my attitudes the ones he would want in my life as a committed Christian? Have I talents that would assist others in knowing the message of Christ if I developed them? Am I using my trained abilities in ways that demonstrate an awareness of Christ in my life?

It is this step which takes your self-analysis from psychology to Christianity. For example, because I am a Christian I have twice in my adult life had to reevaluate myself and move in new directions. In the first case I had grown beyond my beginning adult goals of being a wife and mother. I had also developed as a secure person so that abilities were evident at age thirty-two that were not evident at age twenty. The recognition of counseling abilities *in the light of Christian responsibility* necessitated new training so that those abilities could be used to serve others. The second retraining need arose as I realized that through the activities of college counseling, my "self" now had management abilities not evident ten years prior. These I saw as a gift from God, developed because at the prior step I had followed the Christ expectation.

This Christ expectation is expressed most obviously in the story of the talents (Matt. 25:14-30). Christ expects us to turn what we have within ourselves into more for the honor and glory of God. Hidden within this expectation is the "abundant life" he promised to all those who follow him (John 10:10). The abundance is of the spirit, however, not the paycheck! As you follow the expectation, you develop into a more complete person and as such have a richer return to your spirit from life's experiences.

Since you are a unique person, the Christ expectation will be different for you than for any other Christian. It may lead you into unorthodox paths, places where some Christians might not go, perhaps to people with whom some Christians would not be seen. Christ had the same problem. If your fellow Christians judge you harshly, evaluate their judgment; and if it is truly irrelevant to the Christ expectation for your life, dismiss it. Just remember that in spite of their judgment it is your task to love, to accept their rights and, as Christ did, to claim the same love and acceptance for your self.

Living in the image of Christ is to know your self clearly and then to recognize the possibilities in that self when his image is superimposed on yours. *Liberation gives you the freedom to express that composite image in the world around you as a unique presentation of the Christ-directed life.*

Helps to Development

Along the way of personal and Christian growth you may need some help. Fortunately, it's available! For the development of your abilities, you need look no further than your local adult education program or community college. A wide array of learning experiences is available to increase your knowledge in almost any field. To a lesser extent this is true for your attitudinal development. Classes in psychology, marriage, parenting, women's re-entry programs, assertiveness training—all can serve to help you know yourself.

In the urban community there are mental health organizations, social-work agencies, private counselors, and public seminars. While these may not all be available in rural areas, other resources are offered through your church or local organizations. Study groups, leadership training opportunities, retreats, marriage encounter or enrichment workshops are all chances for you to grow, to increase your personal confidence and eventually make you a more valuable Christian to those around you.

Whenever you take part in these activities, try to keep in focus the Christ expectation: what will Christ want me to do with what I learn here? In this way *every learning experience*, whether secular or religious, becomes a soul-expanding opportunity.

The local church is perhaps one of the best leadership training centers in our nation. Because its opportunities for service encompass almost all human activity, there is always a place for you to develop your skills. The church needs people who relate to people; it needs administrators, financiers, accountants, cooks, teachers, entertainers, musicians, writers, artists, public speakers. Any and every talent/ability you possess can be used—and increased—in your local church. With such increase also goes the opportunity to link with other Christians in the support and encouragement of your faith.

One other resource is available to every person attempting to live the Christian life: life itself. There is no room for fatalism in the liberated Christian walk! You are not a puppet pulled about by Almighty strings. Rather you are a seeking, searching, intelligent human being who struggles to know the "will" or purpose for which God can use your life. We all have choices to make—and a choice about *how* we will make them. This is at once our freedom and our responsibility.

Being free to choose this job over that job, this attitude over that attitude, demands that we struggle with the Christ expectation in all of life's experiences. For example, a person is suddenly confronted with the loss of a spouse. He or she is free to curse God and turn away or to trust God to reveal growth and new expectations. In other words, he or she has a choice of attitude. A necessary change of employment or place of residence gives one the opportunity to wither or expand. The Christ expectation of expansion carries with it the promise and support of inner God resources to meet the new challenges. "God with us" then becomes a meaningful truth (Matt. 1:23).

Living free and living in Christ become synonymous when the Christ empowers us to do the tasks of our prayerful choices, to whatever end those tasks may lead. Living free in Christ is to draw on the depths of his words and promises to lift and lead us through life's crises. *Living free—liberated living—is to walk each day with the assurance that your life and its directions are committed into the power of God and that all the choices you make can ultimately be used to increase the kingdom of God upon the earth.*

Selecting a Life-style

Earlier in this chapter, I said that the liberated Christian may find the basis of his or her choices in a new and/or different interpretation of church tradition and teaching. Aside from the prior discussion of church dogma or behavioral dictates, there is in this statement a direct implication about the selection of a Christian life-style.

Christ provided some clear statements when he said his followers were to be in the world but not of it (John 17), to be "leaven" in the lump (Matt. 13:33), to be the "salt" of the earth (Matt. 5:13). His example was even more pointed: he ate with sinners, counted rough cursing men and prostitute women among his followers, crossed racial lines in his conversations. In short he was *in* the world, *not* hiding in the temple.

He did not, however, forsake the temple. It was often the platform for his preaching. He worshiped there. He was consecrated there by his parents, educated by its rabbis. To the very end of his life he carried on a constant dialogue with the temple leaders. Sometimes he affirmed their teachings; more often he was pointing out the discrepancy between "the law" and the love of God toward humankind. The temple leaders and upright members were often distraught by Christ's refusal to follow their rules and customs. His retort on one such occasion was that there "will be greater joy in heaven over one sinner who repents than over ninety-nine righteous people who do not need to repent" (Luke 15:7 NEB). This was said after eating dinner with a "sinner" in the world.

Through the intervening centuries his followers have retreated into monasteries and preached on street corners, worn elegant bishop's robes and run soup kitchens. Somewhere in this milieu is a life-style that is right for you, *a life-style nobody else has ever lived.*

In every generation since Christ walked the earth the world has been full of turmoil. Our age is no exception. Even as Christ taught his burly band of disciples, so today his message confronts the committed Christian with a call to action *in* the world: to love the neighbor just moved in from another state, to help bind the wounds of a friend's broken marriage, to heal the break between father and son in one's own household.

But our age calls for more. Our neighbor has become the

next country, and the starving child in India—or New York City—is an omen of the future of an over-populated world. The disintegration of a friend's marriage makes us fearful for our own fragile family unit. The broken relationship between father and son may be caused by drug or alcohol addiction or outspoken homosexual choices, forces we don't know how to cope with.

Never has the world so needed Christians who are willing to remain grounded in their faith yet move into the world, laying aside the easy and often pious responses of some churches to the problems around us. Words like "abortion," "civil rights," "women's rights," "homosexuals," "birth control," "eugenics," "space colonies," "test-tube babies" are synonyms today for first-century words about neighbors. The liberated Christian will need to probe deeply to know what it means to "love [my] neighbor as [my]self" (Matt. 22:39). Liberation will demand looking past the *labels* of problems to the affected human beings Christ calls us to love. It may also demand taking an unpopular, and to some an unchristian, stand on behalf of the "neighbor."

In other words, like Christ you may have to go into the world to help heal its problems with or without the agreement and blessing of the whole Christian fellowship, indeed often with their criticism. When you perceive the entirety of a problem and the people caught in its effect, you may have to come to a different conclusion than the popular—and usually simplistic—solution. When you take your stand on that issue *as a Christian*, it is possible you will feel like "the voice . . . crying in the wilderness" (Matt. 3:3 RSV).

So choose your life–style carefully, prayerfully. Study the scripture. Seek the fruits of the spirit (Gal. 5:22, 23). But having put on the "whole armor of God" (Eph. 6:11), having recognized and trained your talents and abilities, knowing your own person and the Christ expectation for you, walk without fear into the midst of the world.

For he has come "to heal the brokenhearted, to preach

deliverance to the captives, and recovering of sight to the blind, to set at liberty them that are bruised" (Luke 4:18 KJV). As you set about bringing the liberty of Christ to others, you will yourself be set free. The liberated Christian life is waiting and the way is clear: *to thine own Christ-directed self be true.*

Suggested Additional Reading

Barnes, Dan. *Extra-Ordinary Living for Ordinary People.* Irvine, Cal.: Harvest House, 1970.

Duncombe, David C. *The Shape of the Christian Life.* Nashville: Abingdon Press, 1969.

Humphries, Jackie. *All the Things You Aren't—Yet.* Waco, Tex. Word Books, 1980.

Lewis, C. S. *The Best of C. S. Lewis,* "Christian Behavior." New York: Macmillan, 1977.

Sumrall, Lester, *Living Free.* Nashville: Royal Publishers Sceptre Book, 1973.

CHAPTER FIVE

LIBERATED, CHRISTIAN, AND SINGLE

It is in the single times of life that the choices we make for ourselves can consume us. We make them alone. We have no one else to blame if they go wrong. Sometimes we have no one to consult to determine how to make our life choices. Singleness is a circumstance of living. The presence of Christ in the inner person, while it may help to combat loneliness, does not change the single state.

Living single and Christian is different from living single without faith and its accompanying moral and spiritual goals, the Christ expectations (see chapter 4). From all three groups of singles which will be discussed in this chapter I have heard the same statements: the potential partners I meet often cannot understand my moral standards. For many single people, picking their way through today's amoral society is an often treacherous task.

But singleness is increasingly a way of life for Americans. For purposes of clarification I see singleness occurring by choice, by default, and by death. Let me state from the beginning that I realize that many of the conditions of life common to one of these categories extends into one or both of the others, just as the marriage patterns we will discuss in the next chapter are not always distinct. They are separated here, however, because there are some major differences with which you may have to deal, depending on how you have happened into your single life condition. So please take from (and add to) all three single situations from your own life. After all, these pages are designed merely to be helps to you in finding your own Christian life design.

Single by Choice

Let's begin where we all once were: young and unmarried. At this point in life, singleness is a choice for some and a waiting for others. Increasingly it appears to be a choice in our society. While marriage is anticipated for some of this group, it is seen as coming after other life experiences such as education, career establishment, travel, and so on. For others it is a life-style choice.

If you are a young single who intends someday to marry, you are faced with a difficult array of choices which begin slightly after junior high school. At this point you probably would not define yourself as single, but rather as a teenager still growing into adulthood. Since our society has no clear "rites of passage," the entrance into adulthood and the single state may come about through your first major value choice: to smoke—and what to smoke; to experience sex or to remain virgin; to drink alcohol or to stay with Pepsi; to go with the crowd or to walk alone when it comes to value choices. And even these choices carry levels of choices within them through which you must move as you mature and take your place within the college and/or working milieu.

Equally important on the young single horizon is the expansion of the inner self. Value choices are, I believe, the reflection of that self as it searches for the correct expression of the inner person. And your inner person is in rapid change. It will be thrust from the familiar world of family to the peer society and finally into adult expectations, all in the space of five to ten years. While as a teen-ager you may be faced with specific acts of choice, as a late teen-ager you are faced with life-shaping decisions: career, education, marriage partner. And in our society we expect all these choices to be accomplished with excellence, although you may have virtually nothing but instincts to draw from—certainly not years of experience.

At the same time adults assume that because you as a young single have little responsibility you are having the "best time of your life." My experience as a counselor working with college students is often in sharp contradiction to this image. You are caught in the expectation of parents to excel, the expectations of friends to conform, intimate relational expectations, and if you are Christian, the expectations of the church and/or the Christ. This is not a time of freedom but a time of testing: pulled in many directions you are beginning to discover that finally a person can only be who he or she is and do only what he or she is personally capable of doing.

To be liberated in such a maze is accomplished in part by the personal inventory and goal setting discussed in chapter 4. From knowing who you are and what you want to accomplish, you as a young single can derive an ideal to aim for. You may not always reach that goal, but through the maze of choices you can keep coming back to "norm up" to your own set of standards.

It is also helpful to have some definition of sin. The legalistic church is often attractive to the young single because it tells them what is right and wrong, leaving no gray or unexplained areas of decision. All "sins" are defined. The problem with this concept is that if the person commits a certain act, he or she becomes a sinner—an outcast to that religious society. Since most of us, young and old, tend to pull away from situations in which we are looked down upon, the natural thing for the young single (or anyone) is to leave the church. If the wound to the self-image has been particularly severe and laden with heavy guilt, it may be

years before there is a willingness to enter into religion
again—if ever.

Yet young singles tend to live with a high level of energy,
curiosity, and sexual tension, which drives them to explore
cultural norms and taboos to *discover for themselves* the
validity of adult judgment. To the older, established
Christian this exploration can be seen as "sinning," since
the pronounced "sins" are acted out. The young single,
you—still in a state of personality development—may be
keenly damaged by such judgmental criticism. And you
may—or may not—be sinning.

Liberation, for the young single, or any other person
trying to live the Christian life, is founded on having
decided for oneself what sin is. The Bible is full of talk about
sin. If we look to the definition of the word apart from its
theological concept we find this: "the departure of a moral
agent from a custom prescribed by society or by divine law
or divine command; moral depravity; wickedness; iniquity;
an offense in general; a transgression . . . connected with
guilt" *(Educational Book of Essential Knowledge,* Consoli-
dated Book Publishers, 1971). In this rational definition we
find heavy words such as "custom," "law," "command,"
"guilt." These are words of legalism, and the definition is
correct whether it is used in society or the church—provided
the faith of that church is legalistic. Yet in Christianity
there comes the voice of the entreating God: "Come unto me,
all ye that labour and are heavy laden, and I will give you
rest" (Matt. 11:28 KJV). These are not the words of a God
with a whip in hand. Nor is the concept of legalism
portrayed in Paul's deliberations with the people at Rome,
when he tells them that they "are not under the law, but
under grace" (Rom. 6:14 KJV).

Paul, however, does not stop with this statement but goes
on to describe the agonizing inner struggle he experiences
in trying to do what he knows he should yet often failing in
his attempt. He even does what he knows he should not. The

salvation of Christ is that finally the sinful self through the gift of God's grace takes second place to the indwelling Spirit, and condemnation is removed (Rom. 6–8).

If we trace back the concept of sin to its origins in the Old Testament, we are pushed into the Creation story, where the perfect human, made in God's own image, commits an act of disobedience and suffers the punishment of being separated from God, i.e., turned out of the Garden of Eden. I offer to you this basic concept as a definition of sin: separation from God. This is not my original concept but is derived from the writings of many theologians. I encourage you to read for yourself and come to your own conclusions about sin. Liberation as a Christian not only allows but requires such responsible searching, since liberation comes in part from using the best of your mental capabilities.

Now let's return to the young single. Suppose that he or she is armed with this definition of sin, which may be translated thus: if what you do causes a break in your relationship with God, then to you it is sin. Along with this definition must come the responsible consideration of tradition and culture, of law and commandment. "Sins," under such a definition, can no longer remain identical for all people. One person may commit an act while another would be hurt by the same act. For example, Lutheran Christians think nothing of using wine in their Communion services or of drinking it with their meals. Evangelical Christians, on the other hand, might view themselves as damned by such an act, since for them it establishes an example for non-Christians that does not measure up to their particular Christian standards.

No wonder if you are a young single you feel confused when experiencing the ambiguity of growth coupled with a maze of differentiated directives each claiming to be right. Your struggle is not unlike the struggle of Paul in teaching the early church. Yet Christ gave a fairly clear perspective to the matter. When the Jewish scribes were quizzing him on which was the greatest commandment (or law), Christ responded by pronouncing a dictum that is above all legalistic concepts: "The first of all the commandments is, Hear, O Israel, the Lord our God is one Lord: and thou shalt love the Lord with all thy heart, and with all thy soul, and with all thy mind, and with all thy strength: this is the first commandment. And the second is like, namely this, Thou shalt love thy neighbor as thyself " (Mark 12:29-31 KJV).

In other words, instead of worrying about what *not* to do, you are concerned with what *to* do—and that act is complete love. When you love someone, you try to nourish the relationship, to make yourself more lovable, to know more about the person you love, to please him or her as much as possible. No one needs to tell you what laws to follow; you will follow your heart. And if the object of your love loves you and encourages you to love yourself, you understand the request to, in turn, love others in the same way. You will not want to break the relationship with the loved one (God) by hurting the "neighbor." You would naturally not steal, rape, plunder, or abuse yourself or others in any way, since this would displease and separate you from God's loving approval, which makes you a full person.

The young single, and any other person trying to live a Christian life, finds him or herself not under law, but under the admonitions of love. Sometimes *because we love* we move across the boundaries of accepted law or moral taboo. Conversely, because we love and are loved we must often stand alone against the encouragement of friends to enter into activities that we know would break our relationship with God.

We, like Paul, must struggle with the *keen conscience— the sensitivity to ourselves, the world around us, the people with whom we are involved, and the Christ-spirit, which we want to make evident in our living.* For the young single this sensitivity provides the guide for choices. It may thrust you into an anti-nuclear demonstration or cause you to take a racially unpopular stand. It may also make you stand against your peers to refuse personal indulgence at the expense of a member of the opposite sex. Whatever choice you make in the world of taboos and social "laws," it will be made with the evident responsibility toward others spurred on by the premise of the demonstration of God's accepting and unmeasured love.

As the young single matures and becomes the young adult single, he or she must establish values for single living. Probably the most flaunted "liberation" concept of our time is that to be liberated is to be sexually free, albeit perhaps not totally promiscuous. This concept is sold by the media as if it was a new discovery uncommon in all generations before us. Another concept is the choice of a career instead of marriage: with one's sex life not subject to marriage, one is free to remain single in order to revel in the joys of work.

This is a very old concept. In Paul's time he found it necessary to spell out his preferences for young Christians (I Cor. 7). He wished that for the sake of Christ the young men would remain unmarried like himself. But he realized that "it is better to marry than to burn" (v. 9 KJV). He talked about the travails and worries of the married versus the single. And he frankly recognized the stresses on both sides, concluding finally that either state is all right for Christians. Paul was writing with the expectation that the end of the world was at hand, and was concerned with the urgency of getting out the Christian message.

Today Christians equally concerned with the urgency of the Christian message may freely choose modes of life like those advocated by Paul. Mother Teresa lives a celibate life and gives her time to the care of the poor—voluntarily. In the history of the Roman Catholic Church thousands of young people have made this choice. To choose a career instead of marriage carries with it freedoms not always available within the matrimonial bond, particularly for women. If a young person decides to remain single today so that he or she can be free for discipleship, the choice follows in the footsteps of tradition within the church.

Yet the pressure to marry is strong. People who are married want you to be like them. The freedom—and the presence—of unmarried people is threatening to the married. It pulls their attention away from their relational commitment and toward their own "missed opportunities." A young couple with children must create time for themselves. They do not have the time or money to dress and travel about as the single career person might. Recognition of this fact causes them subconsciously to close ranks, to point out to the offending single the joys of a close relationship and of parenthood.

Unfortunately there is no need for either single or married to be at odds with the other. The world is big enough for both. There is a joy in being single and pursuing a career. There is also joy in parenting and in an intimate relationship. As in Paul's day, both should be options for Christian expression.

There is an underlying animosity, however: sexual privilege. No matter how many words are written in the Bible or in *Playboy* about sex, the "sinfulness" aspects will always remain with us. It is the nature of the animal kingdom to clearly define the mating partner, and once rights are established to thereafter defend those rights. We still struggle with this instinct of our nature. We write it into our laws and define it in our sins. We provide freedom for sexual expression within marriage not allowed outside the marriage bond. For the single Christian—in college dormitory and in private home—the unanswered question often is: If I go to bed with somebody can I still call myself a Christian? Am I sinning?

Well, are you? Your "keen conscience" answer to your own question will come closer to truth *for you* than any answer a church or sermon will ever provide. For if what

you do damages your relationship with God by replacing it
with a sense of shame, if it separates you from your prayer
life, then chances are you have already determined that
what you are doing is sin. Whether you can still call yourself
a Christian is a separate question. All of us are aiming for
the ideal. None of us has arrived. If you determine that what
you have done is sin for you, then to repair the relationship
with God you will need to ask forgiveness and reenter into
fellowship. To fail to do so will not liberate you by freeing
you to have sex, but put you in bondage by forcing you to live
with your guilt.

Liberation in the area of sex as defined by the
non-Christian world is equated with freedom to choose a
sexual partner at will, to disregard the teaching of scripture
regarding sex before marriage and after divorce or
widowhood, in short to be free to engage in sex for sex' sake.
You will need to read for yourself the teachings of the New
Testament and make your own determination of what is
right for you as a Christian. I would only add some
guidelines derived from working with young adult singles:

1. sex is addictive;
2. liberation allows no as well as yes;
3. freedom from sex can be a positive force.

The first is best illustrated by a young man who came into
my counseling office one day. He was a senior in college, had
abstained from beginning sexual relations because he
believed that as a Christian he wanted to give himself only
to the person he was to marry. He had met such a woman,
had become engaged, and then entered into sex with her.
Several months later they had broken their engagement,
and the young man was, in his words, "ready to go out and
rape every woman" he saw. He did not intend to do this, you
understand, but used the expression to tell how intense his
need was for sexual release once the habit of intercourse was

begun. Only through experience had he come to a complete understanding of the reasons for housing sex within marriage, where the partners are committed to a continued relationship, where the dangers of venereal disease are controlled, and where the possibility of pregnancy is not such an overwhelming threat. For the young single the awakened sexual response has an addictive force and opens the doors to many negative experiences and results which affect the physical, psychological, and spiritual aspects of life.

The second guideline is equally as important. When a person is liberated to make individual choices, he or she may choose to say no as comfortably as to say yes. The media only considers the "yes" choice; yet "no" can be a freeing alternative. As a liberated person you may want to remain unentangled from sexual liaisons simply to stay totally free of inopportune relationships while you are busy exploring other aspects of life. "No" can be a statement of liberation!

And finally, freedom from sex can be turned into creative energy. Often the young single who enters into sexual relations becomes so obsessed with it that he or she can think of little else. If a partner is not available, the pursuit of one becomes disproportionately time-consuming and energy-draining. I have watched this happen to many young college people who prior to beginning a sex life have been campus leaders and involved creative people but whose creative activities drop to a minimum after they have entered into a sexual relationship. Obviously this does not happen to all young singles, nor does sex become consuming for all. I simply offer these observations to help you in making your own choices. Check them out with your friends. Read the scriptures. Pray. And then decide for yourself what your values will be.

Single by Default

To become single by divorce may be your choice or your partner's; in either case it is singleness by default. The sense of having failed to fulfill a contract or agreement, failed to measure up to your own earlier value choices and relational standards is often an accompaniment to divorce. It is easy to think that divorce is always failure; married society tends to think this way. But divorce can also be liberation for one or both partners. Certainly liberation can be your choice of attitude.

Let us suppose that you are the spurned partner. Your spouse has casually—or not so casually—announced that the marriage is over and he or she is leaving. The almost automatic response is that intangible question: where did I fail? Some Christians do not accept divorce under any conditions except adultery. If this is the case, the failure question is often coupled with an equally difficult one: will God forgive me? An excellent discussion of divorce and the scriptural teachings about it is to be found in a book titled *The Asundered* by Myrna and Robert Kysar. Rather than attempt any theological analysis, this discussion will center instead on the aspect of divorce as an act of liberation.

Sometimes divorce frees a partner to become more of a person. When this occurs it may represent the highest act of love the surrendering mate can give. For example, two people come to a point in life where each has changed. They are now so different and have such diverse goals that to remain together becomes damaging to both. They may still share love and caring, but they realize that their togetherness prevents one partner from carrying out an accelerated life plan or some creative possibility. In such a case divorce may be liberating.

Conversely, a person may be left unexpectedly and unwillingly alone. Having to depend solely on his or her own resources for survival, the person is required to develop new skills and expertise with an accompanying growth in self-confidence and inner security. Spiritual growth, taken for granted when the physical comforts were easily supplied, may also suddenly accelerate. Divorce in this case, even though it was unwanted, becomes a liberating force.

In another case one person may feel that the relationship has become destructive to children and self, and the most Christian thing that can be done for all concerned is to put a stop to such harmful forces. By initiating the divorce, self and family are liberated to a more loving, calm life-style.

Is any or all of this Christian? Is it failure? In the sense that the ideals of Christ are not reached, a failure exists. Yet such failure is true in almost every moment of all our lives. Christ recognized this fact when he charged the crowd about to stone the woman caught in adultery to let the one without sin cast the first stone (John 8:7). All of the accusers disappeared, for all of them, like us, had fallen short of the sinless state. We all must struggle to remain in communion with God. To fail is human; to ask forgiveness and depend on God's grace is Christian. To allow the constructive force of Christian liberation to flow through us in time of failure is to allow God to use our failures to complete his glorification within us.

As in every other experience, divorce becomes real failure only when we allow ourselves to become bitter, hating, self-pitying, unforgiving. When through the pain we can pray for the best possible outcome for our ex-partner, can accept the pain as the price of loving, and can commit the outcome of that loving into Almighty hands, divorce becomes success, albeit only in the inner self . . . which may be the only place that success really occurs for any of us.

You may be asking how one goes about loving one who has abused you. To look beyond the act to the person caught in inner struggles is to understand and to love that essential spirit. This is not easy to do when we are in great pain. It is *an ideal to seek after* which our Lord demonstrated on the cross, while he endured ultimate pain for a world that continually rejected and grieved the Creator. In trying to make the ideal come true, you will be ensuring the positive force of love which will bring about your own healing. This is perhaps the ultimate test of trying to live out Christ's teaching, which goes beyond loving one's neighbor: "Love your enemies, bless them that curse you, do good to them that hate you, and pray for them which despitefully use you, and persecute you; that ye may be the children of your Father which is in heaven" (Matt. 5:44, 45 KJV). If you will read all the way to the end of that fifth chapter of Matthew, the concluding verse will tell you that Christ was holding up an ideal.

Sexual choice becomes an area of Christian struggle for the divorced single, as for the young single. What applies now? Do you follow the rules for the young singles, or if your partner is still living do the words about adultery apply? Perhaps you will read the brief statement Paul makes about young widows and conclude you ought to rush right back into marriage (1 Cor. 7:8, 9)! In discussions Christian people who are divorced mention the whole gamut of sexual release, beginning with masturbation and usually ending with a caring relationship. There are no easy answers. Each person must make choices based on who he or she is, who the other person is, and what values they have established for themselves.

Recovering from divorce is a process that may take quite a while. It is a good time to rework your personal inventories described in chapter 4 and to set up for your new single self those standards by which you will now live. When you have predetermined who you want to become and consequently how you will conduct yourself, your decisions will not be made on the spur of the moment but rather you will be liberated to deal with an emotional issue with a straight head.

Divorce and its subsequent choices can destroy you or liberate you. You are the one who decides. For the Christian there is a way, and that way is love; not a physical, erotic, momentary love, but an ideal that remains in front of us at all times to ultimately lead us to perfection, and to God.

Single by Death

To be single by death is to combine loneliness with singleness. When two spirits have truly been joined, the death of one becomes the wounding of the other. In the struggle to bind up so great a wound, it seems we will never be able to function as a complete person again.

Grief is a natural and necessary process. It is the way we are healed. God has built-in recovery mechanisms for all our systems—physical, mental, and emotional. Our responsibility is to allow them to be used by God for our healing. On the way to the cross and death, Christ turned to women weeping by the road. "Weep not for me," he says, "but weep for yourselves, and for your children" (Luke 23:28 KJV). He went on to explain all the things that might happen that would give them real cause for tears and grief. What he outlined is much like the cause of grief that a desolate partner experiences. It is for ourselves that we grieve—for our gaping wound. It is for our loss, our memories, our absence of love, our assumption of unknown responsibilities that we weep. It is for our empty bed in the night—not that of the partner who has left. Unless the death of the partner has come at the height of exuberant life, we have less need to mourn *their* loss than our own.

Yet the grieving for the Christian is tempered for both the one who has died and the one left living. The gift of eternal life, Christ's establishment of victory over death symbolized in his crucifixion and resurrection (Luke 23, 24), provides for the Christian the promise of continued life after death, where there are release from pain (Rev. 21:4), new tasks to take up (Matt. 25:21), and the joy of living in the presence of

God (Rev. 21:6, 7). In these the living partner can rejoice and give thanks.

The living Christian also has resources in scripture to carry him or her through grief. If there is ever a time to soak up the promises of God as given to us in scripture, it is at the death of a lover and partner. Listen to some of the words Christ spoke:

"I am with you alway, even unto the end of the world" (Matt. 28:20 KJV).

"Be of good cheer; I have overcome the world" (John 16:33 KJV).

"If I go . . . I will come again, and receive you unto myself; that where I am, there you may be also" (John 14:3 KJV).

"In my Father's house are many mansions . . . " (John 14:2 KJV).

"I am the resurrection, and the life: he that believeth in me, though he were dead, yet shall he live: And whosoever liveth and believeth in me shall never die" (John 11:25, 26 KJV).

As you immerse your loneliness in the word of God, you come to know that even though you are now single, you are not alone.

What you must do, however, is build a new life—a single life. Your ability to do this may be in direct proportion to the degree to which you have retained your individuality in your married life (see chapter 6). It will also depend on your ability to choose liberation over the bondage of perpetual grief. This is a time for listening to the entreaties of friends to join them at lunch, to welcome their assistance in reentering the world. At no other time is the "fellowship of the believers" so important to your well-being. But remember: people have difficulty reaching out to the grieving, because they feel unsure, afraid that they may cause greater hurt. If you constantly rebuff them, they will cease to ask. Further, they may be waiting for you to give some indication that you are ready to give up grief for life.

This time of grieving is also a time for you, as a new single, to take a personal inventory to help you begin a new life. No matter what your age, you now are akin to the young single who must make his or her own choices—perhaps with interference from sons and daughters instead of parents, with expectations imposed from friends and employers, and with economic responsibilities you may be ill prepared for. While you work your way through the times of depression, you will need to often draw apart to pray and read, to meditate, to learn with Paul that Christ's strength "is made perfect in weakness" (II Cor. 12:9 KJV).

You will find that as you give your weakness to Christ, he will enable you. Slowly the wound heals and you discover that you are still alive. You may also share some of the distress of the single by divorce, the sense of failure. Did you do all you could for the partner who is gone? Is there guilt over things you said? Might he or she be alive today if only . . . These feelings constitute our ultimate weakness which we can only surrender to Christ, for nothing we do now can change the past. If we committed a wrong against our partner, we can only ask God to forgive us and trust his promised grace. Then we can recognize what we have learned from the wrong, so that we will not need to repeat it in the future. Finally, after we have cried out our anguish until we are dry inside, and confessed our failures, we can only be our human selves: someone who has no inside track on perfection, but is as subject to mistakes and errors as anyone, someone who is dependent on God for guidance.

Whether you enter the "singles" world to find another mate or are content to remain alone, your liberation will be found in the acceptance of this new turn of events in your life. Like any divorced single, the widow or widower may choose bitterness and anger toward God, or may move out into a new world and new life. The church can provide for you a warmth of acceptance not always accorded the divorced single, since no failure is implied in the death of a mate, as it is in the death of a marriage by divorce. Married people tend to be less threatened by a grieving widow or widower. You are also likely to find that others who have lost their partners can share the experience of loss, and this sharing can help you to establish new friendships.

As you accept your new state, you can begin to test your strengths and add to them. You may need to retrain for job entry. Perhaps it will be the way you tackle simple tasks like meals that will need changing. You may need to be the one who reaches out to others, sharing your new freedom of time that formerly was invested in caring for your partner. The love you automatically shared must now be planned and redirected, for to lose a partner does not mean that you are no longer capable of loving. It is in the continued giving of love to others whom you seek out that your life will be made anew.

For all singles—young, divorced, widowed—liberation lies always in Christian personhood. Before you are categorized you are an individual. The care and maintenance of your self as a child of God and as a follower of his Son becomes the support system for life in whatever state you may find yourself. When your spirit rests securely in the care of the merciful and trustworthy Creator, you can welcome life with confidence. When you reach for an ideal but fail, you can try anew, or go in an entirely different direction. You can choose values and standards right for your Christ-centered self regardless of whether they fit the norms of the society around you. You can walk through grief and discover the joy of knowing that "we are more than conquerors through him that loved us . . . persuaded that neither death, nor life, nor angels, nor principalities, nor powers, nor things present, nor things to come, nor height, nor depth, nor any other creature, shall be able to separate us from the love of God, which is in Christ Jesus our Lord" (Rom. 8:37-39 KJV). That's what I call liberation!

Suggested Additional Reading

Krantzler, Mel. *Creative Divorce*. New York: New American Library, 1975.

Kysar, Myrna, and Kysar, Robert. *The Asundered*. Atlanta: John Knox Press, 1978.

Narramore, Bruce. *You're Someone Special*. Grand Rapids: Zondervan, 1978.

Reed, Bobbie. *Making the Most of Single Life*. St Louis: Concordia, 1980.

Small, Dwight Henry. *Christian, Celebrate Your Sexuality*. Old Tappan, N.J.: Revell, 1974.

Smoke, Jim. *Growing Through Divorce*. Irvine, Cal.: Harvest House, 1976.

Williams, Don. *St. Paul and Women in the Church*. Glendale, Cal.: Regal Books, G/L Publications, 1979.

Young, Amy Ross. *By Death or Divorce*. Denver, Colo.: Accent Books, 1976.

CHAPTER SIX

LIBERATED, CHRISTIAN, AND MARRIED

Perhaps you are thinking that being liberated is fine for the single person, but not for you. After all you're married, employed, and have ten kids—well two, but it feels like ten!

The house of freedom is within you. It is the choices of your mind which imprison or set you free, not the circumstances of your life. Corrie ten Boom (*The Hiding Place,* Revell, 1971) was free in a concentration camp. Paul was free in prison. And you can be free in your marriage, your job, your parenting if you are free in Christ.

However, to be an actively liberated Christian in your marriage requires more than just a pleasant *laissez faire* attitude, a dreamy disconnectedness from daily life. On the contrary it requires an active, intelligent involvement of yourself and your mate to develop a marriage attitude that expresses the spirit of Christian liberation. This involvement will hopefully never cease, for it is the essence of growth in a healthy relationship.

It is not easy to allow a partner to be free, not nearly so easy as demanding freedom for ourselves. Yet the key to liberation for our selves is found in surrendering to God our naturally possessive attitude toward our mate. It is discovering the word of Christ true when he said that to find your life you must lose it (Matt. 10:39). To receive freedom, you must give freedom. The question is, What does giving freedom mean? To answer that question let us first look at some marriage models.

One older couple I know have it all figured out. He makes the decisions. All of them. Unless, through much hand wringing and begging on her part, he capitulates to her demands. When he does give in, it is forever after her "fault" should anything seem amiss with that particular decision. They are totally dependent upon each other: she for strength, direction and support; he for having all of his physical needs met by his faithful wife-servant. We could say that they live in *dominance-submission*.

This is an ancient pattern of marriage. Those who would preserve it in the "Christian" tradition do so under the scriptural injunction of Paul (Eph. 5:22, 23) when he calls upon women—correction, wives—to submit themselves to their husbands. The husband is the head of the wife, says Paul, and there they stop reading scripture. But the pattern is more than just one and a half verses of Pauline writing. The ancient position of the Jewish wife was always one of submission. Likewise the laws of the United States, which were based on English laws before them, suppose that a wife is the property of the man. Only through extreme struggle is this concept being changed in our society today. Such a pattern of marriage blessed by the church is a perfect example of church teachings that have come about as a combination of sociological factors and scripture. In other words, the dominance-submission pattern is not purely scriptural. It can be argued that it is not scriptural at all.

Paul was writing to the church at Ephesus. In this controversial fifth chapter of Ephesians he was trying to explain how Christians should act so that they would present the best witness of Christian living to the world around them. He begins his exposition by telling the people of Ephesus that they should submit themselves *to one another*, and his total message is that submission should be a way of life within the Christian community for all believers in order to demonstrate to the unbelieving world their concern and love for one another. He then goes on to spell out the ways that this can be accomplished, one of which is concerned with the marriage relationship. The wife should submit herself to the husband, but the husband is to give (submit) himself to the wife in the same way as Christ loved the church and gave himself for it. It is difficult to read this scripture without seeing that some kind of *equal* submission and giving is described here! Christ, in fact, died to give birth to the church. Laying down one's life for another person can scarcely be construed as dominating that person.

This is an example of an area where liberated Christians—male and female—will have to evaluate their choices based on scripture read in context without the trappings of traditions handed down from other centuries and societies. Part of the instructions that Paul gave to the Ephesians is already no longer applicable to our day since we do not now accept the owning of slaves (Eph. 6:3-9). The timelessness of the Bible lies in its constantly unfolding meaning: as humans progress and develop, their understanding of scripture also changes. When they are freed from ancient traditions by new awareness and knowledge, the scripture reads differently than it did in earlier times. To read wisely is a great responsibility of Christian freedom.

A second model for marriage might be called *equal antagonists*. This is the precise opposite of equal submission outlined by Paul. In such a marriage no one is free, since the basis of the relationship is not to always be concerned with giving freedom to the partner but rather with taking freedom for oneself. The end result of such a self-centered approach to living together could also be called separate marriage.

There is much encouragement today for this model in our society. Based on the premise that marriage is supposed to give its participants instant happiness, constant sexual satisfaction, and personal fulfillment, such a marriage is generally doomed to failure from the start. When partners are centered on themselves instead of the other person, they do not create a relationship, and therefore they have nothing from which they may achieve satisfaction. A marriage of equal antagonists may exist regardless of whether both partners work or one is dependent financially upon the other. For example, if both work, each may demand to retain control over the money they make, giving only grudgingly to the payment of mutual bills; or they may carefully keep track of the amount of household work the other partner is doing to ensure that each does his or her exact share and no more. Each privilege granted to one partner must be matched by the other, or an argument can ensue.

Unfortunately, it appears that this type of relationship is not limited to young people of the "me" generation to whom it is usually attributed. Rather it has been my experience in working with emerging women since 1967 that such a marriage may come about as the result of one partner's having been denied a full place in a marriage relationship. As that partner grows, and today it is usually the woman, she begins to demand what is rightfully hers: a share in the decision-making, the right to participate in finances, the right to have homemaking responsibilities shared by the husband. He then, feeling himself threatened, pulls into himself and begins also to make demands. The result is two people living together who now become equal antagonists. It is important to note, however, that when this occurs in an older marriage, the earlier marriage model was not an equal one. Had it been, one partner would not have felt imprisoned by the marriage.

What happens then when a marriage is truly equal, where two people attempt to live in "equal submission"? Once we might have responded to such a question by saying that "somebody has to be the head" or "somebody has to be in charge." I believe this was a "change" answer, one given at a particular stage in the transition of family formation that has been occurring in the last twenty years. Our society had lived so long with all legal and social matters addressed to the man, that it was almost impossible even to think that a couple could live with equal input to decisions. Yet people began to think it—and to practice it. Women began to demand full citizenship in and out of the home. Books began to appear which talked of new marriage forms.

But not for the Christian couple. After all, Adam was made in God's image and woman was put under him. Others countered with comments that woman was made from Adam's rib to stand beside him, not to walk behind him. The "fascinating woman" emerged who was to wait on her husband's every need (Marabelle Morgan, *The Total Woman*), while theologians took on the task of explaining Paul's overall attitude toward women as equals (*St. Paul and Women in the Church*, Don Williams, and Virginia Mollenkott, *Women, Men, and the Bible* [see Suggested Additional Reading]). When Christian women attempted to step forward into today's equal and liberated world, they were, and still are, often told to stay in their place, i.e., in submission to men.

Fortunately, the church is filled with variety. There are churches—those churches we talked about—who are open to self-examination, to repentance and correction. They reread the scripture and began to say that perhaps they had been wrong about their marriage concepts. Others clung more closely to their original position, and their members must defy them or leave in order to follow their prayerful choices regarding marriage.

To be *equally* submissive in marriage is a Pauline concept. To be equal in Christ—in Christ there is neither male nor female—is also a basic Pauline teaching (Gal. 3:26-28). The problem for us today is that this teaching has not been followed in the church, so we must pioneer the constructs of such a marriage. I don't pretend to have them all figured out, but perhaps I can pass along some ways that will help you work out your "equal" marriage.

First, always think of the other person before yourself, whether you are the man or the woman. What does that person want in life? What joys can you give to him or her? How can you help him or her to be more free psychologically and physically, so that he or she may accomplish his or her goals in life? Thinking of the other person first is a basic Christian tenet. What is different here is that one partner does not do all the sacrificing for the other, does not yield all personal goals and ambitions. Rather each encourages the other to individual fulfillment and rejoices in the successes of the other. This basic concept builds relationship.

Second, always accept the freedom your partner gives you. Equal marriage can be negated simply because freedom is frightening. It calls us to grow, to change. It demands new responsibilities. Yet it is in the acceptance of freedom that our marriage relationship also grows. We remain interesting, vital persons, individuals who are attractive to each other. Further, as we accept and use the freedom granted to us by our partner, he or she learns to trust our use of that freedom and is encouraged to give us more. In short, we free each other, and the freeing becomes a source of creativity and growth in our marriage relationship.

Third, as much as possible share the burdens that your partner carries. To be mutually supportive of the concerns of the other person is as important as sharing the happy times, yet much more difficult. We are, after all, very private creatures. Sharing the burden does not mean prying it from the partner, but rather being willing to listen, to weep, to pray, to be one with the other until the burden is lifted. Sometimes we will need to help lift a financial load, sometimes a psychological one, and sometimes a spiritual one. As equal Christians in marriage we will carry "one another's burdens" (Gal. 6:2 RSV).

Finally, remain an individual who must ultimately answer to God for the way you live your life. It is this separate perspective which allows togetherness to exist without smothering one person or the other or both. Nowhere in the New Testament do you find that because you are a woman you will be exempt from the expectations of Christ on your life, or because you are a man you will be able to arrive at the gates of heaven on your wife's religion. Each person must "work out" his or her own salvation "with fear and trembling" (Phil. 2:12). Being married does not remove this individual requirement, not will it remove you from the call of God upon your life.

There are other marriage models than the three I have discussed briefly here. Sociology books are filled with them. I have used these three because the first is still often commended by the church; the second represents either a Christless relationship or a changing and threatened marriage; and the third appears to be the scriptural way to relate to each other—in the first or twenty-first century.

Staying Free While Married

At the beginning of this chapter I said that to receive freedom you must give freedom. The "equal submission" model of marriage is a step toward that freedom, but only if the marriage is built on love that springs from each of the partners. We hear much about love. Some equate it with "making love," which is usually a misnomer for experiencing intercourse with another person—a far cry from the effort really required to make love happen and continue. Others talk about "free love," which is not so much free as it is inexpensive. In equal submission, the term "freeing love" is closest to what I am trying to share with you.

Freeing love allows either partner in marriage to utilize any or all abilities in his or her life. Both are set free to take risks because this love gives them total security: if they risk and fail, the partner will try to understand and will forgive, will love them whatever the outcome. This is a love that can be counted on in success or shame, in wealth or in poverty, in joy and in sorrow. It is, in fact, the kind of love that the traditional wedding vows try to express. Freeing love does not enter into marriage with the idea that if the relationship gets difficult a divorce can always be had. Rather it commits itself to building a lifetime, to *deciding* to love, knowing that ultimately love is a decision. You decide to reach out to the partner or to withold your feelings; you decide to love when he or she is unlovely—or not to love; you decide whether to prefer the other person; you decide to allow your partner to dominate you or to be equal with him or her. These and other decisions are part of the process which will cause love to be a continuous function in your married life. And the very acts of decision form the basis for freedom, for with constant love comes the ability to trust which is the ground of all freedom in marriage.

When each of you trusts the other, when each knows that the other daily decides to give love freely, you are then each set free: you have achieved freeing love. As the days, months, and years of such loving continue, you begin to develop the basis for freeing love which loves forever: joyful love. This kind of love permits you both to move through crises and happy times and remain together; it permits, without the disintegration of the marriage, the stress and strain of individual growth that is not synchronized to the other partner's growth. Joyful love can also bring great pain to the relationship. Because it is so deep, so prolonged, so involved with the intimate character of the partner, it also risks the deeper hurt at the loss of that partner. It risks the deeper hurt of unkind words, of inexplicable actions, or times when the surface relationship falters. But deep, joyful love looks back when the crisis has passed and knows the reward of remaining together, of walking through deep waters and having successfully emerged on the other shore. Joyful love is a forever love and takes a lifetime to develop.

The very basis of such love is the retention of your individual self. This is more than merely seeing yourself as an individual before God. The retention of yourself is based on keeping and expanding your own interests, developing friends uniquely yours, pursuing career goals or education most suited to your needs. The maintenance of the essential self with which your partner fell in love is a major contributor to continuing love.

When two people meet they catch a glimpse of the other's real person. As they move from meeting to knowing, there is a fascination with the character and personality which attracts. Joined in a lifelong relationship, the fascination comes from continuing to watch the other person grow and develop those gifts that offered the initial attraction, a growth that is exclusive to each person. The oft-used example of the partner who achieves a doctoral degree and then divorces the partner who worked to support the two of them illustrates the damage which can occur when only one person grows.

Developing one's talents and abilities is not enough for the Christian, however. The spiritual dimension must also be fed, nourished into maturity, shared as an intrinsic part of the relationship. This dimension can hold great excitement of discovery on an individual and shared basis, and the pursuit of spiritual knowledge and fellowship within the church can provide the marriage with extra strength for difficult times. It can also, however, be the basis of serious divisions between partners.

Understanding Christian Responsibility to Marriage and Self

What does it mean to be a married Christian? To answer that question we must first of all hear the call of Christ

to everyone: "Come to me, all who labour . . . " (Matt. 11:28
KJV). Christ certainly did not specify male or female,
married or single, or any racial group when he gave his call.
At another time he said that "whoever does the will of my
Father in heaven is my brother, and sister, and mother"
(Matt. 12:50 RSV). The pronoun is neuter—"whoever" can
imply male or female gender. The reader cannot escape the
obvious: Christ calls every person, and expects every person
to make his or her own response.

In a liberated generation where women are freed from the
traditional models of mothering and child-bearing, the call
of Christ can place new strains on a marriage. It has finally
become all right to acknowledge that Christ places the
obligation for ministry on women as well as men, that as
equal participants in grace women must also be equal
participants in responsibility. If God calls the woman
partner to ministry and the man to business, the response is
no less important than if the calls are reversed. Yet is it
really possible to maintain a commitment to a calling Christ
and a commitment to marriage, particularly if this occurs
after the marriage has already evolved traditional patterns
of husband-worker, wife-homemaker? Can a woman
emerge into a Christ-called person and be faithful to her
partner?

This is just one example of relationship that demands
freeing love. The question is not so much "can it happen?" as
"will the two people involved allow and encourage it to
happen?" Certainly if one partner refuses the other his or
her growth, the relationship may break. Yet for Christians
there is no room for selfish holding or possession of another
person. Each individual is first God's person, and second his
or her own, and finally the partner's. Even as each shares
with the other, each needs also to share that other with God
in order to set him or her free to achieve his highest
potential.

Marriage is a sociological feature of male/female relationship whose roots are deeply set in religion. In the creation story (Gen. 1:27, 28), we find men and women designed for the completion of each other; but the actual way in which that completion takes place depends upon the society, and runs the gamut of polygamous, monogamous, matriarchal, patriarchal, exogamous, endogamous, and levirate arrangements *(The Interpreter's Dictionary of the Bible*, Vol. 3, p. 279 Abingdon Press). The type of marriage preferred by Christ and the early church was monogamy, one man and one woman joined in a lifelong relationship. Christ speaks to this relationship in Matthew 19:4-9, referring to the Genesis account and upholding for his listeners an *ideal* marriage in which divorce would not be considered. Yet, when questioned about Moses' permission for people to divorce, he goes on to explain that many people were not able to reach this ideal. "For your hardness of heart Moses allowed you to divorce your wives" (Matt. 19:8 RSV).

In an age when marriage and divorce are equally common, when living together is either an alternative to marrige or a trial arrangement, what response is left for the Christian to the words of Christ? There is the temptation to say that Christ was talking to his day, and since Paul proclaimed that Christians are no longer under the law (Gal. 2:16-21) and Christ spoke of the higher law of love (Mark 12:29-31), we are free to overlook the entire issue of constancy in marriage.

Yet the issue of marriage was very important to the early church. Christ's words are also very strong: when two people marry they become one flesh, and no one should separate that union. Paul struggles with the question of the believing and nonbelieving persons who are unequally joined (1 Corinthians 7) and gives special permissions for divorce where such a marriage fails. He also specifies that it

is *his* advice, not God's directive, that he writes to the
church at Corinth.

From it all, however, certain principles appear to emerge
that are as valid today as in the first century. First,
believers should marry believers for the best possible
chance to form a positive marriage. Second, these marriages
should always aim for the ultimate goal of a lifelong
relationship which eventually blends two spirits into one.
And finally, not all people—then or now—are going to be
able to reach this ideal.

In short, even as we all struggle to reach the ideals of
Christian life and acceptance of others, we will also have to
struggle to work out a marriage relationship that ap-
proaches the ideal of spiritual union. We will not always
succeed, either as Christians or as marriage partners. We
then must each decide whether to keep on trying or to admit
that we are not capable of reaching the goal.

In Paul's effort to deal with the unbeliever-believer
marriage, there is a message that we might consider for our
day (I Cor. 7:12-15). In the first century the average life
expectancy was about half of what it is today. Living longer
puts pressures on marriages which were not so evident in an
earlier time. Today there are more changes and stages that
each partner must pass through. These personal changes
are aggravated by an acceleration of change in our culture
through technology and mobility. Our society also abounds
with "change agents": classes, encounter groups, meditation training, sex information and training, assertiveness
training, mid-life crisis seminars, journal keeping, to name
just a few.

To interpret Paul just a little, the result of much of this is
similar to the problems faced when a believer is married to
an unbeliever. For example, two young people marry each
other with all good intention to make a lifelong marriage.
They are compatible, share activities in common, and in the
beginning seem to survive the common growth patterns

brought on by work responsibilities and perhaps parenting. Then one partner takes a quantum leap of growth or turns in a new direction—perhaps a career change, or self-discovery events, or an almost obsessive interest in an area that is not common to both. The marriage is faced now with two people who are no longer alike—a similar concept to the one Paul discusses in 1 Corinthians 7. Where two had a kindred spirit, they now do not. Perhaps they will be able to succeed in continuing to develop a shared life, but perhaps they will not, and if so, they may go their separate ways—without blame. They will have fallen short of the ideal that Christ holds up for all of us, but must nevertheless fall back on the grace of God to accept them as they are—imperfect creatures struggling to become.

For the liberated Christian, there can be nothing less than struggle to achieve the goal, but also nothing less than receiving the forgiving and accepting grace of Jesus Christ when we fail. In marriage, as in all other relationships, we must give freedom and accept its responsibility. As I said in chapter 5, sometimes the most loving and freeing thing we can do for a partner is to let him or her go completely, even to our own pain and suffering and loss—truly an act of loving liberation.

Using Equal Marriage as a Standard

Before such a step ever becomes necessary—in fact before it even becomes a thought in your marriage—the focus of your marriage should be the continued action of freeing love that builds relationship. A *plan* for such action can get you and your partner started in the right direction, a plan you devise.

Start by forming your own Mythical Marriage Pattern (MMP). Each of you should take pen and paper, write down what things you want to mutually achieve in your life together, and then discuss your list with your partner. Go beyond the obvious, such as the number of children, the place you will live, and such. Your MMP needs to deal with the crucial facets of relationship: Do you want to become good friends and if so, how? What place will Christianity have in your relationship and how will the two of you express it as a couple? How much separateness is necessary for each of you to retain your individuality and, conversely, how much togetherness do you need so that you will enjoy your coupleness? What relational goals can you establish, and about what time in your married life do you hope to begin seeing those goals fulfilled? What does "freeing love" mean to you, and how will you express it for each other?

I call this a "mythical" marriage pattern, for it is your dream or myth which can become the mystique of your relationship. It sets up goals and explains expectations. If you choose, your MMP can function as a map, one that will be revised through the years as new territory is discovered and explored in either your togetherness or separateness. Your MMP can also be a sounding board in the hard times when you feel unsure about some part of the relationship, a reference that renews your faith in what you are trying to accomplish over a lifetime of loving.

Your MMP will need revising periodically: after the birth of children, perhaps when you turn thirty—or forty—or fifty—or retire. Each occasion of revision can also be a time of evaluation and renewal, a time to measure successes as well as failures, a time to realize that you are accomplishing some of what you set out to do together. Your MMP can be used as a teaching tool to help launch your children into their relationships and/or marriages. Eventually it can become an inventory of memories shared by two people who never gave up loving each other actively.

Perhaps the best thing about an MMP is that it helps the two of you define your own responsibility to God, yourself, and each other. To return to our earlier example, the woman may feel a calling to enter the ministry, while the man is led by God to use his talents in business. The MMP for this couple may have to begin by setting priorities first to individually follow God's leading, making their marriage or togetherness secondary to this goal. Next they might need to spell out how much freedom each of them will need to accomplish the first priority, and then how much commitment will be needed to nurture their marriage. From this beginning will follow many other questions about children, living habits, and so on, which will clarify how they intend to carry out their primary marriage goals. Ultimately they will define space in their relationship for "you, me, and us," and this definition will help each give the other freeing love.

The mythical marriage pattern of the liberated Christian couple will be based on a constantly evolving concept of equal submission, of loving and preferring the other before themselves, of accepting the freedoms that the partner gives, of sharing one another's burdens, and yet retaining their own individuality before one another and God. The liberated Christian couple will decide daily to love, and in that decision enter into trust which underwrites their freedom. As God loves and accepts each of them, so each in turn will love and accept the other as he or she is, with all blemishes intact but forgiven. They will continually try to express this acceptance and forgiveness in the acts of relationship each day. They will not always succeed, but they will always try. Most important, they will each be responsible to the freedom that comes from the continual trust of a loving and forgiving God, not to abuse it or each other, but to constantly seek new ways to express that love in their world.

The liberated Christian couple will learn through trial and error, through crises and joys, through prayer and fellowship, that it is, after all, the choices of their minds and hearts that define the margins of their freedom. Finally, they will know that it is possible to be married and to be free, free in Christ and in each other.

Suggested Additional Reading

Bernard, Jessie. *The Future of Marriage*. New York: Bantam, 1973.

Dobson, James. *What Wives Wish Their Husbands Knew About Women*. Wheaton, Ill.: Tyndale House, 1978.

Kilgore, James E. *Try Marriage Before Divorce*. Waco, Tex.: Word Books, 1978.

Mollenkott, Virginia Ramey. *Women, Men, and the Bible*. Nashville: Abingdon, 1977.

Small, Dwight Henry. *Marriage as Equal Partnership*. Grand Rapids: Baker Book House, 1980.

William, Don. *St. Paul and Women in the Church*. Glendale, Cal.: Regal Books, G/L Publications, 1977.

CHAPTER SEVEN

LEARNING TO LOVE —PARENTING

Love Complete

Love is a strange demanding word.
At first it seems all hearts and flowers,
teddy bears and warm fuzzies.
And then it changes.

Love begins to demand commitment.

No longer is love self-pleasing
or self-serving—for you or me—
And it makes us grow.

Love grows and then requires our bodies,
Not just our wombs, or lips, but our hands
and feet, our sleepless nights
And it enslaves us.

Love is our captor in the end.
It has taken our selves and given them away,
leaving an empty shell for filling—
And those whom we have loved rush in to fill the void.

Love is then complete.

Equal marriage demands equal decision making. One of the toughest decisions a liberated Christian couple makes is whether or not to be parents. The establishment of a sound marriage in our complex society is hard enough without adding the pressures attendant to raising children. Today no one really *has* to be a parent. Some even view having children as an obscenity in an overpopulated and underfed world.

In this chapter we will explore parenting and nonparenting as Christian options—options for choices only you can make. No individual or church should make this sacred decision for you. The commitment to co-creation with God is among the most significant in a person's life. It should not be the object of doctrine or legislation, yet it is both.

Population control (or noncontrol) is one of the few survival tools of nations and institutions. If a church wishes to expand its ranks, it can do so by denying birth control to its members and thus encourage large families. If a nation wishes to expand its political or ideological concepts, it can provide incentives for birth. Both are current in our world. The irony of the fight to allow each fertilized egg to develop into a human being—whether it is wanted or not—while millions of people starve to death in Cambodia or Thailand is not lost on the thinking liberated Christian. Nor is a nation teeming with hungry people that makes little attempt to control its population. Disposable people make good cannon fodder.

It is against a complex background of hunger, abortion, contraception, inflation, and world unrest (not to mention drugs, crime, and such) that couples today must make their choice to be parents. Once the "choice" was left up to God, for without birth control or medical knowledge, children were born as God "willed." Today we are participators in the will of God, needfully struggling to make right choices for us—and for our neighbors.

The Parenting Choice

Let us first look at some of the results of being a parent on the development of the Christian life. In other words, what does being a parent do for a mother and a father in their search to be one with God? While this may be a self-centered perspective, it is also the one from which most of us procreate. Conceiving a child is an attempt to reproduce our own likenesses, to project our eternal place in the universe. But the choice to have a child carries with it the need for gifts we may not have but which we soon learn the child demands. Those demands can test the measure of our Christian commitment.

Topping the list of gifts that parents are forced to give—and from which they learn in return—is *total selflessness*. While conception may have resulted from self-centered and/or selfish desire, the advent of the helpless child tends to remove even the opportunity for parents to be self-centered, if they are so inclined. Like a great Creative joke, just as our ego peaks and we begin to swagger with self-importance our hormones project us into the search for a mate, and the finding is followed by the arrival of children who immediately begin to eliminate our swagger. One could almost think God planned it so we *have* to be unselfish!

Yet the lesson comes in such a soul-entwining package, gift-wrapped in wonder and tied with awe. With 2:00 a.m. feedings, endless diapers, total dependency, and the first flickering smile of recognition, we are trapped into a lifetime of giving. The child becomes our teacher through its helplessness. "He that loseth his life for my sake," has a whole new meaning as we offer our children endless cups of water (Matt. 10:39). Done to the glory of God, carried out as a participator in the Christ-spirit, parenting can gift us with selflessness.

A second gift is *patience*. From the moment of conception we are put on God's time. We wait: for the child to be born, for its first words, for tentative steps, for schooling to begin, for the first love, leaving home, and finally the completion of the cycle as the child becomes the parent. Yet the waiting never ends, even if it is only for a letter or phone call. Patience is a gift—and a demand—of parenting.

Self-Control is perhaps the most difficult of the gifts to receive. Rare is the parent who has never experienced frustration with the crying infant, the desperation of the groggy mind that wants to lash out and hush the sound. The urge to yell "shut up!" to the child who, only a few short years (months?) before, you were coaxing to talk is a constant temptation. And those are the easy times to learn self-control. As the child becomes an adult who does not accept your life-style and/or values, who chooses a path of self-destruction and defies you to stop him or her, self-control of both mind and body is sometimes the only way to set free the spirit of Christ into the relationship.

Fortunately, another major gift that comes with parenting makes selflessness, patience, and self-control palatable. It is the spoonful of sugar that makes the medicine go down almost unnoticed (as *Mary Poppins* put it in the musical). The gift is *love*. It is not an accident that Christ chose to illustrate the love of God by comparing it to the strongest human relationship, that of parent and child. The picture of God loving the world enough to give "his only begotten son" to bring faith and eternal life to humanity is proclaimed widely not because it was the greatest thing Christ said but because the human race understands it best (John 3:16).

The energy of child love binds us inescapably to our offspring—even sometimes against our own hardened wills. Stories are commonplace in our society of the longing for children given up for adoption in prior years, or parents struggling over visitation rights or child ownership when their marital love has failed. Parents fear nothing more than their child's death or its deformation through birth, sickness, or accident.

Parenting love gives us a clearer picture of a complex God. Christ portrayed God as the parent father and himself as the child son. Such love is an overwhelming but simple statement of the nature of God. We are also represented as children of a heavenly father who cares for us unconditionally, even though he knows us fully and accurately (the hairs on our head are numbered, Matt. 10:30). This picture of a universal parent puts God within our mental reach.

When Christ tells us of God's care and love for us and then adjures us to be like God, the qualities of love spelled out by Paul then become life-style goals as well as parent goals (Matt. 6; I Cor. 13). The Apostle John tells us that "God is love" (I John 4:8). To the church at Corinth, Paul wrote, "Love is patient . . . kind . . . envies no one . . . never boastful, nor conceited, nor rude; never selfish, not quick to take offence . . . keeps no score of wrongs; does not gloat over other men's sins, but delights in the truth . . . nothing love cannot face . . . no limit to its faith, its hope, and its endurance (I Cor. 13:4-7 NEB).

Parenting provides a life stage for the struggle toward perfect love. Every possible test of the characteristics of love can be addressed to a parent through a child. And as there is opportunity for achieving love, so is there equal opportunity for parenting to eventuate in hatred and separation by love's denial on the part of either parent or child.

The choice to be a Christian parent is actually a choice to participate in an enormous life-changing experience from which you—and one hopes your child—can emerge as true children of God, i.e., examples of the God spirit shown to us by Jesus Christ.

Such lessons can be learned through one child just as well as through six. The Christian choice made in view of the world we live in scarcely allows the option of a large family. And for some Christians the choice is to *not* be a parent.

Choosing Not to Be a Parent

In the 1971 edition of the landmark book *The Population Bomb,* Paul Erlich states, "If the pessimists are correct, massive famines will occur soon, possibly in the 1970's, certainly by the early 1980's." Two of his chapter titles sum up the essence of a world in crisis: "Too Many People" and "Too Little Food." As I am writing this sentence, on October 24, 1979, the front page of the *Los Angeles Times* declares a total U.S. commitment of $69 million for the three million people facing starvation and death from disease in Southeast Asia, a famine aggravated by war. A week ago the same paper carried the story of beggars snatching the food from the plates of tourists in the interior of China, along with the admission that hunger is a constantly increasing problem in a bourgeoning population.

Since Dr. Erlich's book was written, the world has witnessed a disastrous famine in Ethiopia, and another in India. Pictures of children with bloated stomachs and great eyes bulging from skeletal faces have become so common-place that they scarcely disturb us as we consume our own three meals a day or survey our bulging, overweight bodies. Our churches often make near citadels of their kitchens, and food and fellowship go hand in hand. "Coffee hours" have become almost as important as worship services on a Sunday morning where one may see well-fed children act positively deprived if there are no cookies within their grasp.

To the Christian who sees this kind of world as his or her *neighbor*, natural parenting may be an unacceptable choice. Even though our nation has sufficient food today, there is no guarantee that we will be able to feed today's children in their adulthood. And if there was such a guarantee, two other specters would still remain: a polluted earth and a nuclear war.

Ironically a part of the pollution of our soil, waters, and even the rains (see "Acid Rain," *Science Digest,* October, 1979) is in large part tied to the need for a constant increase in food production. The use of pesticides has allowed harvests to increase so the world can be fed; but after almost twenty years of their use we are beginning to reap an unexpected crop: disease within human, animal, and plant life. "Carcinogens" has become a household word— and by-product—of this generation.

The nuclear shadow is an even more devastating result of an overpopulated world. In order to find a solution to energy needs on an earth where natural resources are being rapidly consumed, nations have turned to nuclear power. Still in its infant stages for peaceful use, nuclear technology has not yet solved the problem of the disposal of waste materials. Nuclear contamination, coupled with industrial failures, further threatens our children, sometimes before they are born. Further, the war that might be fought over food and/or energy holds the potential for total destruction of our world as we know it. In such an age some people cannot in good conscience bring more life into being.

The liberated Christian who chooses this path may be caught in the cross-fire (an appropriate pun!) of churches that deny them contraceptive measures and/or abortion on the grounds that human life is sacred and not to be denied. The theological tenet that life begins at the moment of conception, along with the ancient dictum of the spirit's entry into the human body, are at the base of the controversy. To choose independently requires a clear knowledge of the basis of choice and a universal concept of loving one's neighbor. When the benefit of the world is chosen above the benefit of one's self, and when this choice is accomplished through prayer and personal struggle, the selflessness taught by parenting has begun in the non-parent.

The Christian choice to *not* be a parent, however, stands apart from the self-centered reasons for childlessness, i.e., a desire for more money or personal time or recreational indulgence. The Christian nonparent choice carries with it an active responsibility concommitant to those which naturally occur in the chosen parent's life. It is also a responsibility that must be faced by the Christian who is childless because of infertility or other circumstances who would otherwise choose to be a parent. That responsibility I will call "being a parent to the world."

The World Parent

When I talked about choosing to be a parent there were four significant "gifts" that emerged from the experience: selflessness, patience, self-control, and love. Christians who choose to be parents to the world—whether they are also parents in a family unit or not—will find the same four gifts awaiting them. By way of illustration, examine with me the experiences of a world parent couple.

Millie and Johnny were very ordinary people by economic standards. He was an auto mechanic who commuted forty miles along a treacherous highway from a rural mountain community to his job in the city. As a young couple they wanted children desperately, but none arrived—until one day a disheveled boy of about twelve wandered into Johnny's shop. After determining that the boy had neither house nor parents, John took him home to Millie. Over the next several months the young couple became his official foster and later adoptive parents. It took a long time for them to replace the boy's distrust and suspicion with love, but eventually it happened. So did something else.

Having discovered a good foster home, the state asked the couple to take a second child—and then another and another. Johnny and Millie decided to move to the mountain area where "their" children could have a healing environment, and Johnny started his daily commuting. He also started building on to the small house they had purchased: bedrooms, an extra bath, a huge living room dominated by an inviting fireplace where family gatherings could occur. Over the next thirty-five years Johnny and Millie lost count of the number of abused children and teen-agers who lived with them, although it was something "over sixty," five of whom they adopted. Several "grandchildren" were born to unmarried mothers who waited out their pregancies in their home while also discovering unquestioning love and acceptance.

Johnny died in 1978. Millie, now in her seventies, continues to keep their home open to their gigantic "family." Out of their inability to become natural parents these devoted Christians became parents to the world in a small mountain community. At the same time, each child was introduced to the love and worship of God through Christ in the church where their "parents" were active members.

Three young men took quite a different tack at being world parents. Companions on a church-sponsored work team to Africa in 1960, they set their individual careers into world parenting. One became first a minister and then a family counselor, helping people resolve the crises of their lives. A second, also an ordained clergyman, found he could be more useful by working with the United Nations to aid the people of Africa. The third pursued a Ph.D. in biology with the intent of eventually affecting the world's food supply. Three unique ministries or three world parents?

Another Christian world-parent type can be found in almost every community. This is the person who makes it his or her task to minister to the sick, the aged, the newly divorced, the neighbor. This person takes literally the scriptural injunction to visit the sick and the imprisoned (Matt. 25:35-46). To some degree anyone can be this kind of world parent, but the childless individual often has more opportunity for such commitment. Additionally, the societal guilt trip laid on the childless couple because of social mores toward parenting dissolve into irrelevancy when world parenting is a consciously acted-upon choice.

Choices in Christian Parenting Style

Selflessness, patience, self-control, and love are not necessarily exclusive to the Christian parent, nor is world parenting. Any moral person can achieve as much if he or she so decides. What makes Christian parenting different is the source from which these characteristics *naturally* come, for it is within parenting that we have the greatest opportunity to demonstrate the complete love of God.

Anyone can give a cup of cold water, or feed a helpless infant. Anyone can visit the sick or imprisoned. *Christ's injunction was to do these things in his name, to recognize and share the source of the love that motivates the act.* This "source" changes these acts from obligation to privileged opportunity. The spirit of Christ within us increases our awareness of other people and their needs, making us long to help them. The recognition of ourselves as children of God creates within us a desire to love and look out for the rest of the family!

Even as Christian lifestyle choices are unique, so will be the modus operandi of parenting our natural children and/or the world. Since there is a child-rearing book written for almost every age of development, and even more books about the needs of the world, we will focus here on the basis of parenting style choices and the patterns they establish in a Christian's life.

As in choosing a lifestyle, the choices of parenting style must be overlaid with the expectations of Christ. For example, a young mother regularly lost her temper with her incessantly moving four-year-old. In a church-school class, she participated in a discussion about using the difficult events of life to show a child the love of God. The following week she reported triumphantly this experience: at the end of a particularly trying day her son had insisted on helping with dinner, thereupon dropping—and breaking—a bottle of milk. Her old anger response welled up. Then she realized this was an opportunity. As her small son trembled and pleaded for mercy, she breathed a prayer, then calmly surveyed the mess. Hugging and forgiving followed, with both of them cleaning up the floor. Mother and son were amazed and pleased at this turn in their relationship. As she related the incident to the class she observed how many times she had innocently rushed to help someone, only to make a mess of it—yet God forgave her. She knew Christ expected her to do the same thing for her small son.

My definition of Christ expectation is as follows: *the choices funneled through our person and circumstances will be those which best approximate the spirit of love and forgiveness taught by Christ.* If we love our children *as we do ourselves* we will weigh each new situation in the light of that love. Asking yourself how you would want to be treated or how you can best demonstrate a loving God to your children can then become the basis for parenting style.

As we attempt to live out the Christ image, we have a responsibility to keep the growing child and maturing young adult cognizant of the source of that love: *to teach him or her faith.* Helping a child become a part of a larger family of faith provides a security that empowers and becomes a resource for independent decision making when the parent is not present. This is not to be interpreted as "preaching" or "facing religion," however; rather it is to developing over the years a home in which prayer and scripture reading are a natural occurrence as are attending collective worship and discussing the faith. Even if only one parent is a believer, the concepts and example of faith can be passed on to the child. It is this essential demonstration and attitude of faith that will cling to the emerging adult long after he or she leaves the family unit.

The same demonstration of love and the identification of its source makes unique our world parenting. Whether within a career or through individual acts in our daily life, to a child or an adult, to a neighborhood or a nation, there comes a time when the liberated Christian seeks to share joyfully the empowering force of the Christ presence. On this small hinge swings the door of Christian invitation to those whom we "parent" or care for. The spoken word of acknowledgment comes *after* the acts of concern, however, making our lives rather than our words the chief witness to the indwelling presence of Christ. Words are sounds without substance unless our acts prove them true.

The choices of a Christian parenting style then are daily ones. They invest the simple acts of life with the teaching of wisdom. They identify the source of that wisdom through the demonstration of love learned from the life and empowered by the presence of Jesus Christ. Forgiveness, acceptance, understanding, loving discipline, empathy— these are all a part of the repertoire of choices available to the Christian parent. They are also the patterns that through the years become as much a part of the parent as of the child, which just happens to be one of the great rewards of parenting!

The Ultimate Parent

At some time in our parenting—whether of our own children or of the world—we must let go of the task. It is one of the most difficult tests of our ability to trust God, to give back totally into God's hands the responsibility we have shared for a major part of our lifetime.

God is the ultimate parent. Out of the God-mystery a child is born. God as our creator-parent moves us from an eternal existence to a temporary or "life" existence. God permits us to leave his control and try our wings in an alien world, a place where as our parent he now allows us total freedom. While in this life we are aware, albeit sometimes dimly, of the mystery of God as our parent, wooing us, reminding us gently of our need to acknowledge his values, to live according to his example demonstrated in Christ. And it is God's hope that we will ultimately want to be reunited with him as we pass from this life back into an eternal existence, that finally we will of our own desire return "home" to dwell in God's presence.

So it is with human parenting. The essence of our selves is demonstrated in our child—or our adopted world child. We invest all that we are into the creative maturation process; then one day we let go. Our child steps into his or her own world. We, like God, must trust the created essence we have imparted to the child and give him or her freedom to live as he or she pleases. We, like God, must trust the demonstration of our love to hold the separated child to us even when great distance or time intervenes. When we are absent from our adult children our love and remembered words may still woo them. Their life choices will, we hope, be made with a consideration of our earlier choices. And finally we hope that they will, of their own free will, want to return home, to seek us out, to be a part of an extended family that includes us, their parents.

How great the responsibility then becomes to found our parenting choices in a loving God, for it is evident that the choices of the parents are visited onto the children, and their children. Likewise, basing our choices as parents on God as our parent model allows us to break destructive patterns that may have been handed down to us by our natural parents. The cruel, drunken, angry, unloving parent can be replaced by our choices to demonstrate to our children or world child a loving heavenly Father, an ultimate parent.

For the Christian who has chosen to be a natural parent, the time of letting go must also be the time of transference to world parenting. The gifts polished by child-rearing are matured and ready to be used in a larger arena. Failure to do so can eventuate in self-pity and a shriveled life. "Go ye into all the world, and preach the gospel" is a *now!* command for parents released from primary family responsibilities

(Mark 16:15). The gospel of love is waiting to be demonstrated in every facet of the world. Whether that world has a three-block or a three-thousand-mile radius for you is unimportant. By sending Christ to this planet, so small among the many places in the Creator's unfathomable universe, God has demonstrated that no world is too small for love.

It is through the continued evolution of Christian parenting that our lives become constantly strengthened and enlarged. Armed with the gifts of selflessness, patience, self-control, and love, we can move confidently to co-create again with God a world that will be healthier and "holier" (more God-like) because we have invested ourselves to its growth and development.

When the time comes that we must finally let go of life and our world parenting, in God we can do so with joy. The return of our spirit to God is truly a "coming home," and the letting go of our earthly family can be done with the satisfaction that our own life has helped establish loving patterns in our world which can be passed on to future generations. We will achieve what every Christian seeks: a life that has made a difference. And we will know that to become a parent—either to our genetic children or to the world—is an inevitable Christian choice!

Suggested Additional Reading

Bennet, John C. *The Radical Imperative*. Philadelphia: Westminster Press, 1975.

Brandt, Leslie F. *Living Through Loving: Reflections on Letters of the New Testament*. St. Louis: Concordia, 1974.

Erlich, Paul R. *The Population Bomb*. New York: Ballantine, 1968.

Skogland, Elizabeth. *You Can Be Your Own Child's Counselor*. Glendale, Cal.: Regal Books, 1978.

CHAPTER EIGHT

COPING
WITH SOCIETY

Come walk with me down an imaginary road lined with nonstop loudspeakers and television sets which bombard us with calls to action. The television images urge us to eat certain kinds of foods, wear particular types of clothing, drink beverages to be acceptable, do this or that job, buy a product. They give us images of what both men and women are supposed to be like and how they are to act, but we realize that the images are not necessarily true. We see that just a few of our fellow-travelers make the effort to turn off the television sets.

As we walk further along the road we notice a multi-national corporation speaker trying to tell us that if we will work for them, do just the right things, wear the clothes they specify, read the correct books and go to the right schools, we can be president of the company some day. But when we look behind the speaker we see a strange phenomenon: many people enticed to enter the door of the corporation are never seen again. Instead, the people emerging from the building look like carbon copies of one another. Only a few enter and come back to the outside world unchanged, their individuality intact.

Yet another loudspeaker seems to project from a church, saying to us: "Invest your time, do good things, serve on the board, cook for a men's club breakfast, be president of the women's group"—and the voice goes on and on. Looking

111

behind the speaker we see harried, tired people running hither and yon with little time to pray. Yet we also see some people inside the church who, though they are working, stop frequently to pray.

On into the horizon we see one image after another, hear one voice after another, all making demands, all wanting us to act. They shout to us: "support the gays . . . adopt a refugee . . . call for the Red Cross . . . walk the block for the United Crusade . . . make money . . . buy a status car . . . " The words blur into a cacophony of sound that drums on our ears until we think we will lose our minds.

Is this really a picture of our world? Yes. It is a world that pollutes us with its demands. We cannot cope with this society by using preformed choices that someone else gives to us. As liberated Christians we would not accept those choices anyway. Yet this incredibly complex and demanding society is our arena for Christian living. Into this twentieth-century world, not the world of 1880 or of 45 A.D., but *our* world, we must bring Christ.

Guidelines for Coping

How do we begin the task of coping with society? How can we preserve our uniqueness, our *Christian* uniqueness, in a society that sometimes seems insane?

To make choices in this society there is one primary guideline: learn to deliberately say yes and no. No matter to what area of your daily life you choose to apply this rule, it will be effective. You cannot always say yes to a child as a parent; nor can you always say yes to a business, a club, or an organization. To be a liberated Christian, however, you must first say yes to Christ and then yes to yourself.

What does it mean to say yes to Christ? It doesn't mean, as we are often made to think, that we must serve on every board and agency of our church. It does mean that before all other demands we put the expectations of Christian living. These expectations are the choices we have already determined for our Christian life-style, which we discussed in chapter 4. They are also the expectations of *time*—for prayer, for scripture, for knowing and waiting upon God. Everything else comes second, including time for ourselves. Yet time for ourselves *does* come second, because to preserve sanity we cannot put time for everyone else before the time we give ourselves. There must be time to care for the body, to keep it physically well and strong; time to nourish it with love and relationship; to give it creative expression that meets the needs of the individual it houses. Christian coping is achieved by saying yes first to Christ and then to yourself.

Sometimes however, you will have to say no to things you want to do for yourself in order to take the next step in Christian coping: saying yes to others. If as Christians we love others as we love ourselves, that love includes equal treatment, which is not always easy to give. Yet to say yes to *Christ* is sometimes to say no to ourselves so that we can say yes to others!

For example, suppose that you get up some morning—barely. You stagger out of bed, pray a perfunctory prayer, wash your bleary-eyed face, and step out the door with half a cup of coffee and a piece of toast in your stomach. You have started the day with a lot of noes for yourself rather than the yeses you need. You have not permitted yourself the privilege of clear praying, nor the privilege of a nourished and awake body. Chances are you will say a lot more noes before the day is over.

This doesn't mean the day *has* to be negative. Because you have said no to yourself about some very important things, doesn't mean you can't choose to deliberately say yes to others. Recognize that you have not done a very good job of getting yourself started. With a heightened awareness of

the negative that goes on in daily life, turn your thoughts
positively to other people. The person across from you in the
office may be having a terrible time. Since you're not having
too good a day either, you can have increased sympathy. By
trying to lift their burdens and saying yes to them, you
discover that you feel better about yourself. Accidentally
you have said yes to yourself. By lifting someone else's
burden, you have also said yes to Christ.

Saying no is among the most difficult of human tasks. Our
desire to be liked prompts a yes answer even when that
answer takes time we actually do not have. Certainly there
are times when we must say yes. But there are also very
important times when we say no. For example, one of the
things that gets lost most in our lives is special time for
relationships. We tend to put all other demands before it,
trusting that the relationship will hold together, when in
actuality the relationship may die because we do not give it
top priority. One need only look at the broken marriages in
our society to guess that perhaps this is occurring at a
greater frequency than anyone would like to admit.

Learning when to say yes and no leads immediately into
the second guideline for coping with society, and that is the
wise use of time. Time is the only thing any of us really has.
Time comes to us free and is dispensed at great cost. When
we rise in the morning to begin a new day, we have been
granted the time of that moment, that hour and that day to
fill or use as we will. And for the most part, only when the
day has been completed do we know what we did with time.
Reversing that order is called for. If you will begin the day
by planning your time, asking yourself what you will do
with it, making a list or planning your time in your
head—or whatever your format might be—you will discover
at the end of the day that you came very close to
accomplishing what you set out to do. So you have managed
your life, as it were, by objectives. You have set out to do
certain things and have therefore done them.

The use of time, or rather its misuse, is perhaps the single most often spoken excuse. "I just don't have time." When you plan your day, and you know what kind of time you really do have, then the phrase, "I don't have time," is not an excuse any more but a reason. If between 5:00 P.M. and 7:30 P.M. you have predetermined that you are going to spend time playing with your children, then when someone asks you to do something between 5:00 and 7:30, you can justifiably say, "I'm sorry; that time is on my schedule for my children and I don't have time to give to you." You don't say it unkindly, of course, but with the sense of knowing that you have chosen the right priorities in your use of time.

The same thing is true in terms of saying yes to yourself. If there is time written in for you to read the scriptures, time written in for you to pray, time written in for you to accomplish the work that you feel is your sharing in the world, your world parenting, then you are comfortable with saying no. You are also comfortable with saying yes, because you know where there is time for you to give away freely and with joy.

The third guideline is one we have spoken of in several chapters: the use of prayer in choosing the directions of life. This is not to say that when you pray God will come down and hit you over the head to tell you exactly what you should do in any given day! Rather, a day started with prayer increases your alertness to opportunities, heightens your receptivity to the events of the day and to the needs of people. When this prayer is refreshed periodically throughout the day, the alertness remains with you. The receptive attitude allows God to speak into your mind, guiding you to opportunities you would not otherwise have thought of.

The three guidelines for coping are easy to remember: (1) learn to deliberately say yes and no; (2) make wise choices in your use of time; and (3) seek direction in prayer. Now let's take a look at some of the pressures in society.

Societal Pressures

A primary pressure in American society is the "ethic" of work. Work gives us our status, economically and socially. Work may be defined as that task to which we normally devote the largest investment of time, and it is surrounded by attitudes which often shape our life patterns. Work is therefore at the top of the list of societal pressures. The intent of the worker and the investment of time are what makes a job important, rather than the existence and/or level of remuneration. The person caring for children at home is working just as importantly as the multi-national corporation employee.

The first pressure of work is finding the answer to the question, what shall I do? This question used to be asked in the late teens, but increasingly it is asked by people of all ages. Career changes are commonplace today, as are career rotations in which an individual stays within the same kind of work but shifts emphasis or position. Sociologists frequently announce that today's young person can expect to have three careers in a lifetime in order to keep up with changing technology. Women are under new pressure to move from the home into careers in the second half of their adult lives. Answering the question of what to do with one's life is increasingly stressful as one grows older, because it often carries the necessity of changing lifelong habits, or of again gambling on the unknown but with fewer years to ride out your luck.

The second work pressure is more daily: dealing with the attitudes surrounding your chosen work. The life of a researcher is apt to be withdrawn; a public relations worker is expected to be outgoing; the social worker needs to care for people. These and other attitudes may assist us in making work choices, since our innate personality traits often attract us to certain vocations. These traits help us cope with the pressures of the job. There are also the specific attitudes of one's corporation. You may be expected to work ad infinitum until the job is done, to meet deadlines that are not humanly possible, to give your life to the corporation first and to put all other relationships second.

Using the guidelines for coping will require you to resist or accept work pressures according to your personal determination of Christian life-style. For example, if an individual says, "I can't spend much time with my family because my work won't let me," he is actually stating that he has made a choice about his use of time. It may be that his or her first priority is the support of the family, no matter how much time it takes; or it could be that the priority is placed on work over relationship. In either case, the important factor is to recognize the *choice* of attitude that either creates or rejects work pressure.

A third work pressure is the need to succeed. Ambition can push us beyond our best and most satisfying capabilities, into a level of our chosen work where we are no longer happy. New pressures occur because we are no longer as competent as we were in a less elevated job. It is difficult to step down, to accept the reality of our abilities. Yet a realistic evaluation includes the recognition that our individual worth is not achieved through work. The Christian's worth comes from being a child of God, not from being president or vice-president. It is better to be a happy tool-and-die-maker well suited for the task than a line supervisor who cannot adjust to administrative responsibilities. It takes a lot of prayer, however, to make such a decision.

Another, more subtle pressure is constantly pushing on the American adult: *pressure to stay forever young.* Listen to the commercials, observe the people who do them on television, look at the advertising in magazines or the styles of clothing designed only for the slender, youthful figure. You will soon discover that unless you dye your hair (or have it implanted if it is falling out), wear contact lenses, keep your figure to a female size eight or a male forty jacket, you are slipping! Thirty is "over the hill"—whatever that means.

This is a most unfortunate pressure because it undermines self-esteem and leaves people feeling inadequate. Prove this statement by your own feelings about a prospective high-school or college reunion. All sorts of images tend to go through our otherwise well-adjusted heads while we try to decide if it is safe to return to the place where once we were very young. The emphasis on youth is peculiar to our society. As a result each of us has the responsibility of formulating our unique attitude toward our own aging process. And the kind of response we make tends to be contingent upon the degree of insecurity within.

We can expect the pressure to stay young to ease as society itself ages, which it will do over the next twenty to thirty years. The great mass of babies born during and after World War II are the predominant population group in our country today. As they move into middle age, we can expect an increasing emphasis on age as a virtue rather than a detriment. Meantime our response to aging will need to emerge out of our own life-style patterns. The statement we make about Christianity valuing all persons, regardless of age, will be read by the world from our personal responses.

Another force with which we must deal today is the pressure upon the family unit. According to the Census Bureau, in 1979 more than 17 percent of all family households are led by women without husbands present, and one-parent families have increased 79 percent since the 1970 census (U.S. Dept. of Commerce News, Washington, August 17, 1980). There is no accurate count of the number of people who are divorced and remarried two, three, or more times, but the words "progressive polygamy" have become a common part of the American language. Each time a divorce occurs in my community, a ripple of fear goes through the married households, each couple fearing that next time it might be their marriage that folds.

Family pressures are legion, including such things as male/female role confusion, conformity to constantly lowering sexual mores, an inflationary spiral that demands both parents work to provide the living, the encouragement of drug and alcohol use, the disregard for traditional institutions and for God as relevant and necessary societal forces, etc. Simply finding time to be together as a family is one of today's greatest pressures.

And the pressures of time are not confined to the adults in the family. Children have become so organized that even their time is at a premium. Little League, Soccer, football, swimming teams, tennis tournaments, plus homework, music lessons, and school activities . . . I think back to my own early childhood and the summers I spent on my grandmother's farm, and I feel very sad for today's children who do not have the experience of running free, of sitting down and observing a frog in a pond, watching a sunset, stepping on a bumblebee and discovering the consequences, of tuning in to the world of nature. Perhaps over-organization of our children is already demonstrating its effect in the numbers of turned-off, apathetic young adults visible in our society. Eventually they do not *have* to be organized, and then they choose not to enter into the organizations of adult society. Apathy? Perhaps. Maybe a well-deserved rest . . .

To resist such pressures on the family, the Christian must place a high priority on relationships and on the preservation of the family unit. The capricious and self-centered love demonstrated on the Hollywood screen must be replaced at home with the *love that is a decision:* you decide that even when the going gets tough you will continue to love. Your sex life may wane, your career goals may change, your children may leave, illness may raise its ugly head, but love can remain—if you choose not to withdraw it!

A pressure unique to the Christian comes from the church. While the church offers a place for fellowship, study, and strengthening of relationships, it also must survive by drawing on the time of its members. Since it meets endless human needs, it in turn has endless needs for helpers. The danger is that because it is the church the Christian will feel guilty if he or she does not reply personally to all—or as many as possible—of its needs. It is essential that you find a place in your schedule for helping in the church. But to assume every task offered is neither necessary nor helpful to yourself or the congregation.

But, you ask, how do you say no to the church? First, remember that the church is not synonymous with Christ and his demands upon your life-style. It is an organization with Christian intent, some of its programs being necessary and some not. Armed with that understanding, you can next say yes to those tasks that really fit your life priorities and through which you feel you can make the most significant contribution to the church. This frees you from guilt. Then say no to everything else. Each time a request comes to you, weigh it in the light of what you are currently doing, the time it would take from other parts of your life, and the expression of Christ it might add to—or subtract from— your life-style. To assume too much denies others; to assume too little denies yourself. More than one Christian has lost track of their inner direction by substituting church work for Christian living. Saying no is often the best Christian choice!

A final significant pressure in today's society is the tension between the sexes, and more specifically, the confusion over the role of each sex. What is a man to act like? Can a woman be feminine and a feminist? Should a father be active in the parenting relationship—should he change diapers and do household chores? If the mother works, should she feel guilty because she ought to be at home? If she is at home, should she instead be working outside? These sex-role pressures must be handled on an individual basis, because no satisfactory role development has emerged in our society.

Strong statements are being made by churches today about the place of a woman. Some simply state that a Christian woman should stay at home and raise the children. Does this mean that any woman left as a single head of a household cannot be Christian if she goes to work to support her family? What kind of conflict does such a statement create in a woman who has also been told by her church that welfare is dishonorable and work honorable? In the "battle of the sexes," peace reigns when each individual gives every other individual the freedom—already given them by God—to work out their own salvation, to evolve their own Christian life-style in a way that best makes them a demonstration of the Christ presence. The gifting of such freedom should be a high priority in the liberated Christian's life-style.

Between married partners, role change for one implies a need for personal change for the other. *This ongoing transaction must be kept current.* Love begets love. True love sets the object of love free to be him or her self.

For example, if the wife works because there is a need for added income in the family unit and her job takes the same eight hours a day that her husband also works, the Christian demand of caring for each other will require life-style changes in their approach to household tasks. When these changes are based on an examination of self as a demonstration of Christ in a relationship, there is no loss of femininity or masculinity.

The changing of roles demands the extension of the ways in which we show our love to one another. Whether those changes destroy or enrich our marriages depends on the responses we choose to make, from taking out the garbage to cheering success on a new job. It has always been so in marriage. The only new pressure is whether you will choose to feel personally blighted if you make a role change and your partner does not change with you—in the way society says he or she should. The change is your choice; the reaction to that change is your partner's choice. If the changes you make exceed the coping ability of your partner, you will be faced with the need to evaluate your priorities once again: what is more important—your continued change or your relationship? Society will tell you that it is *your* change, *your* career, *your* freedom that should take precedence. As a Christian, however, you will need to ask the deeper questions of love, perhaps to see even your partner as your neighbor whom you should love as yourself. Loving may just be more important than living according to society's standards!

Priorities, Limitations, and Responsibilities

It is not enough to talk about guidelines and pressures without also realistically assessing our limitations and responsibilities. Only in this way can we establish priorities for ourselves that make sense. I have said that one person cannot do everything that is asked of him or her. It takes courage, however, to say to a company or church that you have made a list of priorities for your time and what they are asking simply is not on it!

All of us have limitations. Our bodies require certain amounts of sleep and food. Times of quiet, rest, relaxation are essential to the life of the psyche. To the extent that we really *need* (require) such expenditures of time, we are limited. Responsibilities, on the other hand, are tasks that we must do regardless of our limitations. If I am a parent I must take care of the child. If I am a worker I must complete the work. Only after we consider the limitations and responsibilities real to us can we make choices about the rest of our time. We have been discussing coping skills which involve making choices that have to do with parenting and work. Prioritizing those choices has to do with limitations and responsibilities.

For example, if you are married but the only partner in the marriage who is active in the church, you will be limited in your participation. To not limit yourself is to deny the relationship of marriage to which you have committed your life. When the scripture suggests saintliness as a way to bringing an unbelieving partner to Christ, it is not talking about always being absent from home because of business in the church (I Cor. 7:13-14). Such overinvolvement, in fact, presents a negative image to the unbeliever, because the church robs that person of a love relationship rather than building one. Both responsibility and limitation are involved in such an instance, and both must be considered in coping with the pressure to volunteer.

Up to now we have been talking about priorities of daily life and the use of time. These are closely tied to the life-style goals discussed in chapter 4. The coping guidelines are applied on a daily basis to make your life-style emerge as you have prayerfully established it. There is a second level of priority setting required for coping, one that reaches far beyond daily considerations: *the establishment of life-long values that you will adhere to no matter what happens.*

Suppose that you establish honesty as a part of your value priorities. To achieve honesty requires making it a daily goal. But prior to the daily goal must come the long-term priority commitment that allows you to attain the goal. The pressure from your work may encourage you to lie when you have not quite completed a job. The prior commitment never to lie will keep you from it—or at least make it unpleasantly difficult. Perhaps you choose not to drink. Given a high priority that choice will enable you to withstand the societal pressure to drink. You can say to the pressure, "That is not in my set of priorities!"

As a Christian you can resist pressure because you are not doing it by yourself. In the first place, we are talking not about becoming merely a moral person, but rather choosing a life-style that demonstrates the Christ presence, and resists anything that does not belong in that demonstration. As a Christian you choose to establish priorities in prayer, and the strength to sustain them comes from God. You will, in fact, have some priorities that non-Christians might not consider. You could decide to make Christian joy a way of living; then you would need to express and be involved in the evolution of joy when the pressures of society are strong upon you. Perhaps you set prayer and scripture reading as a part of your life-style choices; now you make time for them a priority, because they are essential elements of your value system, and are your base for action.

Whether limitations and responsibilities affect value priorities, only you can determine. Since none of us is perfect, you will probably find yourself succeeding in your resolves one day and failing another. You might, for instance, find yourself lying to keep your job. Later you realize that if you had been a little stronger in your belief, God could assist you in your chosen life-style, and you would have been able to resist.

There is a way to acquire that God assistance. Once you have established your priorities, take a final step: turn them over to God. What an easy statement! What a difficult task! This is an act similar to committing your life to follow Jesus Christ. The act of giving your priorities to God carries with it an anticipation of empowering, a strengthening from within to carry them out. When you fail, you pray for strength to succeed the next time, and gradually your successes outnumber your failures. Paul called it "pressing toward the mark" (Phil. 3:14 KJV).

Sometimes the pressures of society are so heavy that we think we cannot handle them. Turning through the pages of the Old Testament we hear the same kind of lamentations from Job, from David, from Isaiah. "O Lord, have mercy on me" was their cry. Today they would probably say "Lord, help! I cannot cope!" But now, as then, the conclusion would be the same: God is still in his heaven, God is still good, God will sustain. Turning over your priorities to God gives you the same power that the Old Testament prophets used; the same power Christ called on when he prayed, "Let this cup pass from me" (Matt. 26:39 RSV). His was an agonizing choice, yet following the Father's will was his top priority. And the strength came. Strength enough to sacrifice life itself . . .

There has never been an easy era in which to live. There have always been wars or rumors of wars. There have always been earthquakes, famines and floods . . . and murders, muggings, kidnappings. People have ever been tempted to lie, cheat, steal. The only real difference between our age and those before it lies in our knowledge of the entire world. The pressures are magnified by our awareness even as the world shrinks.

In this expanding world of awareness, liberated Christians must be able to say yes *and* no, based on the priorities they establish through prayerful consideration. They must make wise choices in the use of time. The values of life must be established so that daily actions reveal the Christ presence. And finally the liberated Christian needs to turn over his or her priorities to God along with the success and failure faced in coping with society.

Coping is the ultimate translation of the New Testament statement: "I can do all things through Christ which strengtheneth me" (Phil. 4:13 KJV). And the best part is—you really can!

Suggested Additional Reading

Dunn, Charles V. *The Upstream Christian in a Downstream World*. Wheaton, Ill.: Victor Books, 1978.

Hansel, Tim. *When I Relax I Feel Guilty*. Elgin, Ill.: David C. Cook, 1979.

White, Jerry, and White, Mary. *Your Job: Survival or Satisfaction*. Grand Rapids: Zondervan, 1977.

CHAPTER NINE

LEARNING
TO FEEL

In the struggle to cope with all the pressures of life, it helps to be in tune with your emotions, for they are the music of the soul. Played out in daily living, they allow us to express the hiddenness that is our selves.

But to be "emotional" has fallen into disrepute in civilized American society. If a woman weeps she is a hysterical female; if a man touches another man in love his motives are suspect. Actions based on feelings are unscientific and therefore questionable. If decisions cannot be rationalized intellectually they are considered misguided.

For the Christian especially this poses a dilemma. Prayer is an emotional act. It is an effort to expose the inner person at a feeling level and to allow those feelings to be incorporated into our total life structure. Prayer is also an act of opening our intellectual self to a force that we cannot rationally explain. We "feel" the results of such activity and express them in emotion-packed words: empowered, renewed, strengthened . . .

In addition, the basic Christian command is an emotional one: love one another. Christ did not instruct us to think through the human need around us and to take specific actions. Instead he told us to love and assumed we would figure out the right things to do. In the Book of Acts we read about the early Christians sharing their wealth, caring for the widowed and homeless, expressing love among the

Christian community (Acts 4:34, 35). To the me-centered person of our era this must seem a weird way to live!

True liberation, however, implies a freedom from the norms of convention and a responsibility to understand why people act the way they do. The conventional "stone-faced men" and "hysterical women" are role descriptions derived from a long history of behavior.

The settling of our nation required a toughness of mind and body, an endurance of hardships beyond today's comprehension. The strong, silent man who bore up under adversity was a desirable role model for survival. The model changed slightly as people moved west, and the silent man augmented his emotionless face with weapons to increase his physical strength. A man was expected to be the *actual* protector of the home. There was little room for frivolity, no room for tears, and love was verbalized infrequently in this model which we receive from history.

Women, on the other hand, had much to cry about. They bore many children without the aid of today's medical knowledge. Many of those children they also buried, victims of disease and pioneering. Women suffered through menopause without hormonal therapy or knowledge of what was happening to them. Now there are pills for every time of life! Without them it is conceivable that many people would not run on as even an emotional keel as is expected in today's world.

The remnants of these patterns are still with us in child-conditioning. Often we hear a parent advise a little boy not to cry, because boys (or men) don't cry, while his sister is petted and loved when she sheds tears. And while tears are only one evidence of emotional relief, this patterning causes the male to internalize emotions and the female to externalize them, each conforming to societal expectations and patterns.

Liberation from these patterns carries with it the delicate task of accepting one's emotional self as an essential ingredient of the personality. To be aware of the love we feel and be able to express it in thought, word, and deed—openly—is to take the phrase "God is love" and make it active in life (I John 4:8). Through our caring, God becomes real to people who know us.

Being emotionally aware is more than knowing the good: it is also tuning in to our negative emotions—our greed, our hatred, our anger. It is being a whole person with both constructive and destructive parts. For the Christian it is also standing before God with all our parts bared knowing that there is a purpose for the entire creation that we are.

Knowing Your Emotional Self

Just as it is necessary to open yourself to an examination of talents and abilities, to evolve goals and life values, so is it essential to confront the emotional person you are. Since a great deal of spiritual impetus arises from our deeper self or subconscious mind, we need to be aware of the emotions through which it must pass in order to be played out in our everyday life. For example, suppose that you are a person normally satisfied with life and your possessions. But then you begin to want more than you have. All around you are people who have what you want, but for some reason that you cannot explain, you are denied increased material wealth. You work hard, you increase your education, you do all the right things that should bring you more wealth, but still you remain with only limited possessions and money. This begins to be a fixation that soon affects all of your thinking: you are possessed by greed.

Since this has been a slow process, you are perhaps unaware of what has happened within your emotional structure. Others may see it, but you would deny this characterization if confronted, forming all manner of rationalizations to support your frame of mind. In this state, your praying and reading of scripture would probably tend to deny the existence of greed, since you deny any change within your self. The expression of the purer emotion of love, which ordinarily would spring from your spiritual self as openness and warmth, is now filtered through your desire for wealth, and your love may be subconsciously withdrawn from those who do not cooperate to help you achieve your material goals and be given instead to those who do. Without confronting and ridding yourself of this damaging emotional state, you will be unable to express the pure love of Christ to all people.

Or let us consider something less long-range and complex. You are at home caring for a new baby, a baby long desired and welcomed with adoring love. But you are tired and worried. You have received a phone call from your husband in which he has suggested that he might lose his job. The baby is fretful and crying, so that you are prevented from getting quiet within your self, and your worry mounts. Finally it erupts as anger toward a child who will not hush, and you change its diaper with rough movements and put it in its crib to cry alone. Anger and worry have temporarily shut off the deeper emotion of love.

So it is that we must do at least three things in order to deal with our emotional self: (1) identify and/or confront our emotions; (2) separate the positive and negative emotions we possess for quick recognition; and (3) establish outlets for both positive and negative emotions. In this way we will be able *to use our emotions with control* instead of either burying them or being controlled by them.

Identifying Your Emotions

It's time to get out the paper and pencil again. This time, list all your *actions* toward other people. Jot down all the emotions you *usually* exhibit with each action, as best as you can recognize them. Next examine your *thought* processes when you think about life and your relation to it. Here you may find emotions you hide that are not on your first list. Be totally honest. List every one you can observe in yourself.

After you have listed the emotions you can easily identify, go back over your actions and thoughts and list the emotions that occur only occasionally. When you write these down, also put on paper the circumstances that evoke the emotion.

What you have now is a list composed of the following: emotions acted out and emotions only felt and thought, with those most often experienced at the top of the list under each category, followed by those felt less often. Write across the top the words "Outgoing Emotions."

Now take another sheet of paper or turn that one over and write at the top "Incoming Emotions." We both give and receive emotions, and our actions evoke various responses from others. Your incoming list should begin with the names of people from whom you receive some kind of evident emotion. It may be a very specific feeling or something more vague, almost indefinable. Put it down, even if you are not sure you are correctly naming the emotion.

When you have exhausted your ability to see your emotional self in this manner, share your list with that trusted person who helped you back in chapter 4 or with someone who loves you enough to be kind but honest and knows you well enough to be objective. Let that person add anything to the list that he or she deems important. Then discuss the order of the very first category: the emotions you think you demonstrate to others. Find out if what you think your actions show really is felt by others. If your friend sees the emotions you have listed in a different order of predominance, ask him or her to write out the order they perceive. Then try to discuss the differences gently but objectively. Remember when you enter into such a discussion that the object *is to listen*, perhaps take notes, and talk about yourself as if you were some other person. In this manner you will be able to eliminate the attitude of defense or rationalization that will cloud your self-perception. In other words, this is no time to let hurt feelings (emotions!) deafen you.

Positive and Negative Emotions

The next step can be done with or without your trusted friend. On a third sheet of paper establish two categories: positive and negative. Carefully go over each of the emotions you have listed and ask yourself: does this emotion leave me feeling better or worse about myself? If better, then put it under positive, if worse, it will go under negative. When you have finished separating the emotions into the categories, set aside the positive list for a while.

Examine each of the emotions on the negative list and *write down exactly* what that emotion does to you. Does it make you act differently toward someone, and if so, whom? In what way? Does it change the way you speak or act generally to all kinds of people? Does it make you withdraw a positive emotion you would otherwise give? Is it one of those emotions that is evident to you in your thoughts but not in your actions, perhaps, an emotion that you are suppressing because you are afraid to act it out lest it hurt you by damaging your reputation, or hurt someone else to whom you have intellectually chosen to be kind.

Now look at your repertoire of positive emotions. Choose which ones you might be able to substitute for *each* negative situation and write down some alternate behavior that would enable that positive emotion to be demonstrated. Now put away the lists after one last reading.

What you have done is sensitize yourself to the way you are acting and thinking emotionally and the effect those emotions are having on your everyday life. You have gained considerable knowledge about yourself. But knowledge without practice is dead, so determine to spend the next two to five days being aware of your emotions as you go about your regular everyday activities. You may want to carry around a note pad so that periodically you can write down your observations. And remember to record emotions given and *received,* for this way you will come to know what evokes certain emotional reactions toward you.

At the end of your observation period you should have a pretty clear picture of your emotional self. It is possible, however, that you will find yourself with such a complex picture that you cannot take the next step alone. In that case find yourself a professional counselor, or refer to your trusted friend to help you proceed. Read on and then decide. . . .

Establishing Emotional Outlets

"Rejoice with those who rejoice, weep with those who weep" (Rom. 12:15 RSV). Paul spends a good part of the twelfth chapter of Romans talking about ways to use emotions forthrightly. He concludes his admonitions with one of the best prescriptions for emotional health ever written: "Do not be overcome by evil, but overcome evil with good" (Rom. 12:21 RSV). In modern language we might say, "Don't let your negative emotions control you, but replace them with positive ones."

To be a liberated Christian is not only to be able to express our emotions, but to also be constantly striving to be free of negative emotions. In short, to replace evil with good. Or to turn the power of a negative emotion—one that is damaging us—into the power that makes us stronger persons.

You may have noticed that when you separated your emotions into positive and negative, you did so by determining your reaction to the emotion—and the circumstances under which you felt that reaction. You were *not* asked to list good and bad emotions. Had that been the request, you might have put down anger, pride, lust, and so forth on the negative list. Yet anger rightly directed is what moves people to solve the social ills of the world; pride is often the force behind self-preservation; and lust—like the word or not—is frequently the force behind a healthy sex life in marriage. It is therefore impossible to term any emotion negative until its effect has been determined, *for all emotions hold potential for good!*

To arrive at the good, however, you have to go back to that basic injunction to love your neighbor as yourself. You probably have had to put on paper some things you don't like about yourself. That's normal. We all have feelings, thoughts, emotions, actions that we wish were not a part of us. Dislike becomes the impetus for improvement if we let it. And recognizing what we dislike is the first step toward changing ourselves to someone we will like. After all, it is very difficult to love your neighbor a whole lot if you don't love yourself at all!

What would it mean to really love your neighbor? First of all, you would need to forgive them all their faults, to accept them just as they are. Are you willing to do that for yourself? Christ is. To show them that you loved them, you would want to approach them with kindness, to sympathize with them when they grieved, to rejoice in their joys, to help them express their anger in constructive ways, to allow them to speak out on issues important to them. Can you do as much for yourself? Part of establishing emotional outlets is to love ourselves at least as much and in the same way that we would try to love our neighbors. Yet often we deny ourselves needed freedom of expression and the acceptance of the person we actually are. We are either unwilling or unable to participate in the Christ acceptance of the spirit dwelling within us because we get it so muddled with the body in which it is housed and what society tells us that body should be. Scripture directs us to be beautiful in spirit, and society tells us to be beautiful in body. Scripture tells us to put on the armor of God; society suggests Christian Dior. Scripture tells us to lay up treasures in heaven, while society wants us to buy real estate. Our task is to let the scriptural injunction be supreme within our spirit, while providing adequately for the body without letting it have first place. It is in this fashion that we achieve internal peace and self-acceptance.

For example, if we look upon the spirit of a person instead of the body we are forced to concede that the color of skin is unimportant. After all, what color is a spirit? If we love the spirit, the essential person, how can we be put off by a twisted body—or a foreign accent? Or poor clothes? Or gender?

To love the neighbor—whoever he or she may be—as we do our essential self, our spirit essence, resolves many of the negative emotions we daily experience. Supposing that you are driving your car and you are caught between a truck bearing down on you from behind and an elderly couple driving ahead of you below the speed limit. You have a range of choices: You can fear the truck bearing down on you; you can curse the elderly couple ahead of you; you can pray for God to protect you; you can enter into a slow boil that will make your driving responses erratic; or you can understand the needs of the trucker to meet deadlines and the pressures he lives with, while admitting the slowed responses of the elderly and their need to live within their limits. You can acknowledge their kinship to you as children of God. You can be aware that your essential self is in God's hands and that whether physical harm comes or not is therefore somewhat irrelevant. And in such a calmed state of mind you can remain alert to the opportunities to safely extricate your automobile from its position on the highway. Loving your "neighbor" has been substituted for anger or fear which could diminish your judgment.

Maybe on your negative list there is a person who always irritates you at work by talking when you need to work. Rather than expressing your need—which is the kindest thing you can do for them and you—you suppress your anger until one day it boils over and you alienate them entirely. This one entry on your negative list may in fact be a symptom of a much deeper problem you encounter regularly: you don't feel strong enough to express your needs on a continuing basis, so that an outburst of anger is the only release you have. Assertiveness training courses can help you learn to express your self so that outbursts become unnecessary.

When we follow the scriptural injunction to love ourselves we are assured of our individual worth as children of God *who have something to contribute* that can help the whole human race. And equally important, we can accept the other person's worth and contribution. Our task is to learn to express ourselves *before* anger erupts. If that is impossible we need to be able to say to the unfortunate person who receives our anger that we are sorry, that we have not yet learned how to say what we want and need until motivated by anger. The intensity of the anger comes from that inability as much as, or perhaps even more than, from the incident that evokes it. People *by themselves* do not make us angry. Anger comes from *our* inability to deal with people when they obstruct our activities or needs. We are really angry with ourselves, with our helplessness or lack of courage.

A genuine love for our neighbor allows us to deal with the anger, the helplessness, the fear. For love turns the question from "What will he or she think of me if I express myself?" to "What is the best thing I can do for this person and myself in this situation; what would be the most loving thing to do *for*

both of us?" Fear replaced by love yields courage and
eliminates anger and helplessness.

Your list holds specifics that cannot be addressed here. It
is at this point that you may need to enlist the confidant or
counselor to help answer your questions: How can I
eliminate or deal with this attitude? Is there a way to
resolve the frustration of this situation? How can I break an
old pattern of aloofness to let the freedom of love shine
through? By examining the negative emotions and circumstances under which they occur, you can begin to evolve new
channels of expression, new ways of dealing with old
problems, of turning the negative emotion into a positive
one.

Relaxed in Love

*Finally there is only one thing left to do: to relax in the
supportive love of God,* aware of your own emotional
structure and ways of becoming free to express your inner
self. This is not to say that the task of confronting your
emotional self is done forever. No task of the spirit is ever
complete, for life constantly forces us into new growth by
placing demands upon us we have not previously experienced. There is however a security, a new kind of trust in the
Creator, which emerges after such an in-depth discovery of
self. This security will carry us through new periods of
growth, reassuring us that we can meet this crisis, and the
next.

Unfortunately, security can also be our deterrent to
growth. We become so confident that we lose the very
sensitivity which propelled us into self-examination. Our
emotional patterns grow comfortable, and we no longer feel
the need for change. Then when our life situations change,
or the people change to whom we bare our emotional life the

most, we continue to use the old patterns without consideration of the new demands.

Love never ceases to demand. If it does not continue to expand and shape itself to the needs of the loved one, it ceases to be love. Our love for God yesterday is insufficient for our increased understanding of God today. Yesterday's loving action will not meet today's crying need.

So we are faced with a constant duality: *being relaxed in the love of God requires that we constantly expand our spirit to encompass the needs of those whom God presents to us to love.* We can never close the process of self-examination and understanding; yet we cannot linger over it or we defeat the process.

Nevertheless the acceptance of the emotional person we are allows us to weep with those who weep, to rejoice with those who rejoice. We can pray freely without apologizing to a society that does not understand. We can put our arms around a fellow child of God and comfort him or her. Because the love of God has shone upon us we can reflect that love to a dark and angry world. We are liberated from ourselves— our emotional selves—to be the living example of peace as persons of good will.

Suggested Additional Reading

Hart, Archibald. *Feeling Free.* Old Tappan, N.J.: Revell, 1979.

Peale, Norman Vincent. *The New Art of Living.* New York: Hawthorne Books, 1937, 1970.

CHAPTER TEN

LEARNING
TO REJOICE

Today I had a sign that God was at work. I saw it in a box of strawberries plump, red, and juicy—just like they are supposed to be. They arrived in the market at the precise time of year when strawberries usually ripen, in their traditional recognizable form. When I tasted one—and then another and another—they tasted just the way I remember strawberries tasting. Strawberries in spring are God in a creative splurge! And so, while stemming the berries, I thank God for such a delicacy.

My daughter-in-law stopped by yesterday. She is seven months pregnant with our first grandchild, and the baby is strong and kicking. What a blessing! Not just to have a new child in the family, but to have it in a dependable pattern, shaped like a human with a heart to sustain its life. And what a blessing that our son and his wife want to have a child, that somewhere deep within them has been planted a desire to continue the human race. It is a blessing also that they have no wish to overpopulate the world but only to replace themselves. And so, while talking to my daughter-in-law, I thank God.

The phone rings—a friend has stopped at my husband's office and wants us to have lunch with him. This interrupts my work plan for the day, but I go anyway. While we talk he shares some ideas that fit perfectly into the material I am writing. Another sign that God is at work!

I stepped into the shower this morning and turned on the faucet. Not only did water come pouring through the pipe, but *hot* water, something much of the world does not have. I remember the tiny stream of cold water that ran from a rusty pipe in Somoa, and I thank God for the hot water. It rains, and I thank God for a dry roof. The snow falls, and I can thank God for a warm house, and for warm clothes and dry boots.

I find myself stranded on a busy highway, but because someone has cared about others enough, there are call boxes along that highway and I can reach help. I can thank God for the inventor, the telephone, the help that will soon arrive, for the fact that it is not raining or snowing, for a strong body and spirit that allows me to move through the experience without giving into desolation at being stranded.

Do you want signs and wonders to prove that God is at work in the world? They are everywhere. Just as you learned to love, learned to share your emotions, learned to know others, to be a Christian in all places, so you learn to give thanks. Without a doubt, learning to "rejoice evermore" (1 Thess. 5:16 KJV), is the most important and rewarding learning of Christian living. *It is the key to liberated living.*

Earlier I said that the house of freedom is within you. To be liberated from the negative, angry attitudes of life sets your spirit free to become more than you ever thought possible! When you are constantly looking for ways to be thankful, ways to rejoice, it is impossible to cling to dark emotions. The longer you live with the positive part of your self and look for the positive emphasis on life around you, the more loving and accepting you become, i.e., the more liberated.

Seeing the signs and wonders is only the beginning point. Expressing your gratitude for those wonders to God and others is the next step. How can you dislike people if you are looking for the good in them, and have decided to share your discovery of good with them? For example, the person at your place of work who has a habit that annoys you. You can deliberately search out a good quality in this individual and, having found it, praise him or her for it. Not overdoing it, of course, but simply sharing a good word with the person. Almost always the response is gratitude, often followed by some token of friendship. By keeping that positive image of the person foremost, by thanking God for that feature in the person, you soon find yourself forgetting the unpleasant habit because the individual is no longer a stranger. Friendship replaces criticism, and both of you become richer spirits because of it.

The simple act of saying thank you is another door-opener to freedom. It is easy to say thank you for a gift, slightly more difficult to thank someone for a compliment, and even harder to thank someone for sharing a thought or bit of humor. Yet each of these forms of gratitude has the effect of enhancing the relationship between you and the other person. When a compliment is returned with "Thank you, I'm glad you enjoyed the song I played," the person giving the compliment is rewarded, for the gratitude has been accepted. To tell someone that "I really appreciate your sharing with me"—honestly, sincerely—is to open doors to a deeper and continuing friendship. Saying thank you to a child, to your lover, to the grocer and the shoe repair person, is to give to *them* an expression of your feeling about them or their work. It frees you just a little more than before you said those "magic" words.

But why spend time on such a childish concept? Didn't we learn to say thank you when we were children? Perhaps. But as we mature we tend to say it less and our spirits seem to shrivel in direct proportion to our attitude of gratitude. If you cannot find something to be grateful for in the small things of life, how will you be able to find joy in life's struggles?

Finding Joy in Struggle

Gratitude comes from within. It is not an act that you put on for your personal adornment. When God dwells within you, and you recognize that joyful presence, all you need do is release it to those around you. This is a form of what some call "Christian witness"—a nontraditional form, since it has nothing to do with asking people if they are "saved." It is rather the expression of God shown through you in society.

Being grateful is easy when everything runs smoothly in life. But what do you do when the first gray hair turns into a dozen or they all fall out? Can you be thankful when you fall and break your leg? When the greatest sorrow of all, death, strikes your household, is there reason for gratitude? Are you not, after all, allowed to mourn and to weep like other humans?

This short period of existence which we call life issues from God and returns to God (see chapter 7). Being a Christian in this life is acknowledging the presence of God and nurturing that presence even while we are separated from our Creator Parent. We become the living illustration of "God with us" (Matt. 1:23). What occurs in this life then takes on a different perspective for us than for those who live unaware of the presence. Since earthly life is a process of development in an eternal progression of our spirit, the gray hair and broken leg are accidents of our "house" in which lives the Spirit of God. They do not affect the person within unless we lose our eternal perspective. When we focus on the "house" in which we dwell, each of the trying events of life becomes a downer, cause for great mourning.

And what of death itself? If you have lived all your life in a fine home, have watched it age, have shared its memories and hidden yourself in its special places, you will mourn when it finally falls to the demolition crew. So it is with the body. As humans we mourn the loss of vitality in a dear friend or parent and weep when the body is laid to rest. Yet as Christians we rejoice that the person who lived in the house has moved away to a better place, a place of Being that is limitless, painless, not concerned with the troublesome issues of this world (John 14; Rev. 21:4, 5; 1 Cor. 16:35-58).

Just last week I stood by the casket of a relative and studied the waxlike face, beautifully prepared for all to see that the sting of death is not so bad. As on so many other similar occasions, I was struck by the emptiness of the body. The spirit that had dwelled there had moved out. We who had come to mourn were left looking at the old house, now deserted, remembering the happy times we had shared with the person who once lived there. At that moment I could rejoice that for this person there would be no more pain of the body but rather freedom in the Spirit. The house was worn out and ready for discarding, and we could not be sad at its destruction knowing that the individual had moved on into a new "mansion" promised by our Lord.

But what of all the other times in life when we struggle to blend the body and the spirit into successful living? How can rejoicing help them?

To answer those questions, I'd like to suggest three concepts: turning disappointment into progress; using thankfulness as a way to mental and emotional health; and maintaining a balanced life as a joyful Christian.

Turning Disappointment into Progress

"Rejoice in the Lord alway, and again I say, rejoice" (Phil. 4:4 KJV).

Rejoicing is not always easy. Sometimes it is done with tears streaming down your face. You have failed a major examination, lost a longed-for promotion, had a special luncheon with a friend canceled when it was the only light in your week, your child's behavior falls short of your goals for him or her. The list of disappointments in life goes on as long as life itself. Disappointment can be said to be a condition of life, born out of its opposite condition: hope. Without hope we could not live, but with it life becomes harder.

Paul recognized the anxiousness of our days when he spoke of rejoicing. He immediately follows his admonition to rejoice with a direction for Christians not to be anxious but to turn everything over to God in prayer (Phil 4:6). The constant care and provision of God for the individual is a consistent theme throughout the New Testament. But nowhere is this pictured as some careless abandonment of the trials of life. Rather the choice for Christians is to trust God to bring them through these trials, to work out the purpose of their days, and because of this trust they are able to rejoice. The total surrender to God of your life, i.e., everyday events, allows you to look past the disappointment and/or sadness of the moment and to trust the long view, the overall plan that God working with your spirit can activate.

For example, even as I write these pages I know that in just a few weeks our family will be moving from the place we have called home for nine years. Our roots go deep, and it is a wrenching experience that we had not anticipated at this point in our lives. Yet what an outpouring of love we are receiving from our Christian community! We have loved deeply and the pain of separation is hard, but without it we would not have experienced in just this way the expressions of caring in which we can rejoice. We can choose to mourn or to rejoice. We in fact choose to weep at leaving and to rejoice in what has been here and what will yet be in our new home. We choose to experience freely the emotions of sadness and parting with those we love, yet also to help lead them and us into anticipation of the future that God has for us and for this community. We rejoice "in God" because God places the spirit of rejoicing within us.

Thankfulness as a Way to Mental and Emotional Health

Rejoicing is the healthiest thing you can do for yourself—even if you have to contrive it without the indwelling presence of God to help you! Every time you open your eyes to a new day you are instantly adrift on the unknown. Probably you have some kind of a plan for the day which may be much like the day before it: eating breakfast, going to work, eating lunch, and so on. Sounds boring, right? Maybe you long for an earlier time in your life when you could take off for the beach or the ski slopes and simply revel in living. But today's routine is life too. The daily grind, some call it. For the Christian, life can become the daily opportunity.

Before you get out of bed you can thank God that your eyes open, that your hearing works (if it does, of course), that your hands are attached at the right place on your body—you can even give thanks for the absurd: that your hair stayed attached to your head all night . . .! As you stumble into the bathroom you can give thanks that your body works properly without your prodding; thanks for the shower and the *hot* water; thanks for a dry towel; thanks for clothes to wear; thanks for food to eat; thanks for transportation to work; thanks for money enough to use that transporation; thanks for a job; thanks for a brain to do the work assigned to you; thanks for co-workers who can help you when you don't know what to do; thanks, thanks, thanks. Even as you learned to pray without ceasing (see chapter 2), now you learn to rejoice always. *And when you are constantly involved in thanking God for the minutiae of life it is very difficult to remain depressed, self-pitying, cantankerous.*

You can even make rejoicing an art form. Looking for creative ways to express gratitude in life allows for an expansion of creative thinking and doing. Two years ago I fell into a deep depression, something I had never before experienced. I realized that all the good advice I had given people as a counselor did not hold. I knew the answers: get out with people, volunteer for some service to others, join a supportive group, and such. But in my depression I could do none of these. I could not trust myself. I cried out to God for help and yet the depression stayed. I turned to the medical doctor, who pronounced me healthy, and yet the depression stayed. For three months the tears flowed almost unchecked, triggered by the least persuasion, while another part of me fought to regain control of the always before stable self. I would go to church and get up and leave during the service because of tears. Then I would withdraw further because I did not want to inflict my pain on others or further embarrass myself. The problem was quite simple: I had spent four intense years preparing myself to work in a particular field only to find myself unable to get a job and remain in the area where my husband and family lived. It seemed an unresolvable conflict, and I did not understand why, when I had followed God's leading from the first, the outcome was an apparent disaster.

Finally, in desperation, I remembered what was missing from my life: rejoicing. But there seemed nothing to rejoice about. Creativity was called for, creative rejoicing. It began with the little things I have just described, the daily things. Then followed the option of rejoicing in nature: the hills outside the kitchen window, the green of the spring grass, the flowers growing wild and untended in the back yard. Pushing open the door to the outer world a little wider, my spirit lifted as I could rejoice in friends who had stayed by me, counseled and listened; a husband who had loved me when I was unlovely; children who, though mystified, continued to express their love. All of these I had not seen when I was in depression, when I was wrapped up in myself—which is probably the root cause of nonmedical depression.

Finally, as normalcy returned, I could look back and thank God for the depression: having experienced it I would always be better able to help others through difficult times. The problem did not change, was not immediately solved, but my attitude became positive through praise. The condition of my spirit progressed in direct proportion to the level of thankfulness I was able to achieve in each day. In short, my mental health returned to normal.

Rejoicing can also affect your mental and emotional health, if you will thank God *in advance* for those actions and solutions which lie ahead of you and over which you now have no control. Another way to express this concept is to say that you trust God to secure your future, and trusting, give thanks—whatever that future may be. Earlier we talked about seeing life through the long view. When your life is completely turned over into God's keeping, you can then move and act with confidence, for you know that *whatever the outcome,* God will be present with you. It is, after all, the absence of inner power that we finally dread; our inability to make decisions or to take actions in response to our environment. When God is in control, even powerlessness is nullified as a fear potential, for when we are without power, God is not. Living under such a promise removes the fear of the future. "Lo, I am with you always" (Matt. 28:20 KJV) is perhaps the most powerful promise ever made to humans.

But how does one actually take hold of such a concept and use it in everyday life? Tomorrow I have a job interview. The job is an exciting possibility which appears on the surface to fit many of the things I enjoy doing. This morning I awoke remembering that it would be a good thing to look up the publishing efforts of one of the persons who will be interviewing me. This was a "gift" thought—one of those that is present in my subconscious which surfaces when I awake. I recognize this fact and give thanks for it. Then my mind turns to what I shall wear, but at the same time I know that the task for this day is to write, that this is important in order to reach my deadlines. I turn to God for guidance, and the scripture recommended to you in this chapter sweeps across my mind—don't worry about tomorrow—and I remember that God is with me, directing the choices I make, but that they can be made tomorrow and need not therefore interfere with today's immediate work. I also know that friends are praying for me to be confident and centered in the will of God for my life when I go to the interview tomorrow. I know that I have given ultimate control of my future to God, and that whatever the outcome, God will use it for continued personal growth and for Christian witness.

Therefore, trusting God for the most fulfilling outcome, for clarity of thought and ability to make decisions, I can move into tomorrow without worrying about it today. I will, however, do my part intellectually and physically to prepare for the interview, and therefore set time aside to do this without relinquishing today's work. Having done my part, I can rest assured that God will do his part. Even if on arising tomorrow I find myself stricken with illness so that I must cancel the interview, I know that God is present in that action, provided that I have not deliberately sought out the illness through subconscious fear for the purpose of avoiding the interview.

I make the last statement cautiously, for people often do not distinguish between an acceptance of just whatever happens as the will of God, and the creative best which God holds out for your life. Praise is an attitude that helps develop the "creative best." God wills for us wholeness, health, freedom of spirit, love. We often settle for less than that because we cannot believe that life should be more than the typical human condition of misfortune, accident, sickness, trouble. Our task is to take hold of the promised wholeness and to work with it through care for our bodies, our minds, our spirits, and through projecting into the future the confidence gained from the presence of God in us—in our physical house as well as in our spirit. Part of that projection is the gratitude attitude that allows us to offer praise in advance for the outcome, knowing that doing our best we are also working in harmony with God's best.

As in other areas of life, we may not always reach the ideal. Ultimately our spirits may not always remain strong as our house begins to deteriorate. We may fail some days and succeed others. Yet always we can try again to remain focused in the providing love of God, and thus be set free to move confidently about in the world knowing we are not alone. We can rejoice, for God is truly "with" us, and in so doing keep our minds healthy.

Maintaining a Balanced Life as a Joyful Christian

Long before holistic medicine became a social concept, true Christians knew of its existence. Some even practiced it. Listen to the words of Paul in I Thessalonians 5:16-26 (KJV):

> Rejoice evermore. Pray without ceasing. In every thing give thanks, for this is the will of God in Christ Jesus concerning you. Quench not the spirit. Despise not phophesyings. Prove all things; hold fast that which is good. Abstain from all appearance of evil. And the very God of peace sanctify you wholly; and I pray God that your whole spirit and soul and body be preserved blameless unto the coming of our Lord Jesus Christ. Faithful is he that calleth you, who also will do it. Brethren, pray for us. Greet all the brethren with an holy kiss.

Ringing through these words is a wholeness of life; learn to pray, to rejoice and give thanks, to set your and God's spirit free, to listen and learn, yet decide for yourself what is good for you, to keep away from those things which separate

you from your Creator (i.e., sin), to be filled with peace, to
pray for one another, to share your love with others, and
ultimately to know that God will preserve you blameless!
Not just a physical you but your entire self.

This book has concerned itself with these concepts—but
also with another which is equally important: the acting-
out *process*. Life in our century is different than in Paul's,
but people are the same. Even as we today struggle to find
our way as Christians, so did the people of all the ages before
us. And we have the same guidelines to go by. The
differences lie only in the society around us.

It has never been sufficient for Christians to hide
themselves away to pray. It has never been sufficient for
Christians to let their bodies rot from disuse so that they
were unable to participate in physical life. It has always
been impossible for Christians to seal off their emotions,
their thoughts, their dreams, their ambitions—because
Christians are first, last, and always human beings while
they are in the physical dimension. Like all people they will
have laughter and tears, joys and sorrows, happiness and
despair. They will lose jobs; make money; be pro golfers;
clean streets; play football; read; tend libraries; work in
factories; eat—just as non-Christians do. But Christians
will engage in life while trying to maintain a balance in
which the mind, the body, and the *spirit* are equally tended.
It is from such balance that wholeness comes and from
which joy and thanksgiving flow. To tend only the mind and
body is to negate the God-given strength and peace which
permits joyful living.

Christians are not exempt from criticism. On the contrary
they are frequently the targets of criticism—from an
unbelieving world without and a judgmental self-righteous
populace sometimes found within the church. It is for this
reason that each Christian must work out his or her own
salvation, albeit with great care; or else he or she may never
come to the freedom that allows one to be a unique

expression of God in society, a freedom that brings liberation and joy.

Liberation and Joy

Scripture promises us that "in quietness and in confidence shall be your strength . . . " (Isa. 30:15 KJV).

Three freedoms naturally result from confidence and joy: the freedom to be yourself regardless of your age or situation; the freedom to be a unique Christian; and the freedom to love everyone around you. When you are filled with confidence because you have entrusted your life to God, it follows that you will increasingly be able to—and need to—be responsible to the spirit that dwells within. Likewise, when you have searched out your faith, analyzed and established your personal life goals with their Christ expectations, when you have learned to experience your emotions and share them with others, you will have become a spirit/person whom you can trust. In other words, you can trust yourself through the maturing processes of trusting God. When this occurs, you can be a free person whether you are sixteen or sixty. And because you love other people completely, they also give you the freedom to be yourself.

Remember as you read that last sentence that freedom always has responsibility. It will try never to overstep the boundaries of another person's freedom unless moved by intense conviction and calling of God, which is rarely the case. As we claim the freedom to be, so we must give it to those around us. Nevertheless, joyful personal liberation occurs as the life of the Christian progresses, for fear is removed—fear of others, of situations, of the future, and of death. How can we help being joyful?

The freedom to be a "unique" Christian brings joy as we are liberated from the confines of traditions, of narrow minds and churches, of harsh criticism, and find the ability to study objectively each of these confinements until we reach our own responsible conclusions. We need no longer be threatened by excommunication or imposed guilt, because we know that our faith, while guided by the church, is ultimately a condition between ourselves and God. It is to this relationship that our responsibility kneels, and from it that our joy comes.

And best of all, as Christians we have what the world never gives: the right—yes even the responsibility—to love *all* our fellow humans. Such a right allows us to move among all races and classes of people knowing that we are all the same: all of us are individually in need of answering for our lives before God. We are freed from bigotry; freed from snobbery (economic bigotry); freed from religious separatism; freed from greed, fear, hatred. And we are freed *to* acceptance, *to* classlessness, *to* tolerance, *to* contentment, *to* joy, *to* love.

For this is finally the message and commandment of joy: that we love one another even as Christ has loved us (John 15:12); and that we should love God with our whole heart, soul, mind, and strength and love our neighbor as ourself (Mark 12:30, 31).

And from such love will flow thanksgiving and rejoicing. So, with Paul, I say again to you: rejoice!

Suggested Additional Reading

Lewis, C. S. *The Joyful Christian.* New York: Macmillan, 1977.

CHAPTER ELEVEN

THE LIBERATED CHRISTIAN

By now I hope you have decided what a liberated Christian is. Paul is responsible for the original idea. In his letter to the church at Galatia he wrote: "For through faith you are all [children] of God in union with Christ Jesus. Baptized into union with him, you have all put on Christ as a garment. There is no such thing as Jew and Greek, slave and freeman, male and female; for you are all one person in Christ Jesus" (Gal. 3:26-28 NEB).

What a glorious message to come from Paul's pen! He goes on to recognize in the next chapter what we seem to have lost track of in our rush to defend the status quo: that we live in the Spirit. Here is the essence of our life. We are beautiful, raceless, genderless children who have the capacity of mirroring the true Spirit of Almighty God. It was never Christ's maleness or race that Paul or other New Testament writers extolled. It was instead his Spirit and the teachings and acts that issued forth from that Spirit. It was likewise not the Holy Person that Christ promised to send to us, but the Holy Spirit. The message of the New Testament *is* liberation: from race, from gender, from law, from the bondage that humans impose upon themselves. It is a message of liberation to become whole in our spirit and our relation with the Creator, illustrated for our human understanding by a person with a whole Spirit who as spirit was with the Creator before the world began . . .

Today the church has become divided and punitive along the lines of physical categories: race and gender. It pretends to be united on another division: economic class. Certainly what we term "life-style" is another category that divides Christians, whether that life-style is a variation on activities or on the greater conflict of heterosexual versus homosexual choices. As surely as Christ wept over Jerusalem, he would weep over the church today. It is fortunate that we have had so much time to attempt understanding of the scripture and his teaching, for it is obvious we have just begun to glimpse the possibility of meaning hidden within. We are a divided people unable to decide and to agree on the concepts of faith—or even if Christ was the Son of God, for the word "son" carries an exclusive male property. We cannot see past our social/cultural conflict to recognize that the Jewish, male body was only a house in which dwelt the ultimate exemplification of the eternal Spirit: sexless, raceless, without economic class, a Spirit that remained apart from the sexual conflicts of the body and thus remained totally free from our most separating categories. It is the expression of liberation in Christ that I have attempted to delineate in these pages. There are, however, some fundamental concepts that will assist a Christian in liberated living. First is the one just mentioned: that *we worship God in spirit*—our spirit in communion with the eternal Spirit. It is within the spirit that the concept of faith exists. It does not necessarily exist within the church at large or the local church in which we worship. For the second concept is that *the church is an organization,* a vehicle established by people to assist the message of Christ. Unfortunately, through the centuries it has often presented itself to the world as if it were the message! Not so. The message dwells within us, the people who come into the church. *We are the vehicles of faith.*

The third concept follows logically from the conclusion of the first two: if it is we who carry the message of faith, assisted by the communion of the Spirit and the assistance of the church, *it is also we who must dissect the conflicts of our times to see clearly what is truly spiritual and what is cultural.* And not just of our immediate times, but the "now" along with its connected past. For example, the struggle of women to be equal legally with men is a cultural struggle tied to a long history of legal inequality. That it is an issue in any of our churches is the result of a theological history permeated with ancient cultural influences that result in pronouncements of dogma quite different from the quality bestowed upon women by Christ and the early church. The raceless, genderless spirit called in faith cannot be bound by human pronouncements based on "earthly" cultural categories. Nor can it stand by and allow the church to continue to measure—to judge—the relationship and calling of God upon a life on the basis of such categories. Being male or female, black or red, yellow or white, rich or poor—none of this should enter into the relationships of people in Christ, nor should it be a part of the religious institutions to which they turn for assistance. But since in actuality the categories exist within the church, the liberated believer in our generation must separate what is truly spiritual from what is cultural.

Finally, then, *we must also recognize who is our rightful judge.* In the "world" or culture, we are bound to abide under just laws and to work to change those that are unjust, to make the world a better place for humankind. Within ourselves the judge of our faith is God. The church is after all, an organization within the world which we will not take with us into eternal life. As right as it may be, it cannot be our judge. The church may choose to be our law instead of the vehicle of the freed spirit in Christ. It has that option. But we also have an option: to live by the New Testament injunction that only God judges. This is a much harder option, for church rules may be fairly simple to follow, with scant binding upon our lives and activities. To kneel in submission to the all-searching power of the Holy Spirit is a much greater act, which engenders a pervading sense of responsibility in living.

Four things then: to claim the worship of God as a spirit; to recognize that we, and not necessarily the church, are the vehicles of faith; to separate the spiritual from the historical/cultural in examining the conflicts of our time; and to answer first, last, and always to the singular judgment of God.

And how does this free, you may ask? Does it not place the individual in greater bondage than before, constantly tracked down by a Supreme Being just waiting for a misstep?

When you yield your spirit to God, it is received as a lamb brought back to the place it belongs, saved from all the negative forces that could destroy it, by the loving compassion of a gracious God. That grace becomes your fortress, your safe place that carries you through all the struggles of life. From that grace you can draw spiritual strength, the essential strength in life—in fact the force that we call life. To give over your spirit without thought of gender, race, economics, or denomination at once frees you from those constraints. God and you are simply together sharing strength, direction, purpose.

From such unity you receive the sense of worth that everything you do in this life and all the parts of yourself are created to give glory to the Creator. *So long as you do not break the unity of Spirit you are free to live, free to serve, free to explore all of your world—* in it, but not of it, as John might say (read I John). Furthermore you are free to respond to the guidance of God as you carry out the mission of your lifetime. No one can say to you: you can't do that because you are black or because you're female, or because you're poor. For you know that in Christ we are all equal—one in unity with the Holy Spirit.

You are also free to stand back from the cultural conflicts, from a quarreling country or church, and independently come to conclusions that are positive answers to the call of God upon your life. This does not free you from the *words* of the church or the country, but rather frees you to *examine* those words and to determine for yourself through searching the scriptures, through prayer, through intellectual discovery, what you will accept. Your conclusions must be harmonious with your relation to God and your understanding of the call to present God to the world, else you will not remain free.

And finally, you are freed from the judgment of people. You are always responsible to *consider* their judgment, for they may be far wiser than you; but acceptance or rejection of their judgment lies directly within the scope of your prayer life and awareness of your self as a worthy spirit before God.

In short, *you are freed—liberated—to become all that you can possibly be within the guiding empowering presence of God.*

Before you shout "heresy!" and proceed to tell me where the end of such thinking may lie, let me clearly say that what is proposed here is always freedom balanced with responsibility, speaking with listening, understanding with study, searching with prayer. It is only the old predictable outcomes that are challenged: race, gender, economic class, church pronouncements and judgment.

To be a liberated Christian in our day is to exercise the power of God in each individual life in order to obliterate those categories which divide us, to bring us at last to a place where we will live up to Paul's beautiful words: "all one [person] in Christ Jesus" (Gal. 3:28 RSV).

Not everyone will want to be liberated. It is a condition of humanity that we arrive in life at different stages of growth and remain in the widest possible varieties throughout our lifetimes. Liberation takes courage because it challenges safe places, safe ideas, safe theologies. Some will prefer to stay safe. It is, after all, easier. It also allows one to savor the taste of judgment upon the challenger, the chance to play God.

Others will not want to be liberated because they will see no need for it. The status quo, the old ways, the traditions, become comforting life patterns. They eliminate ambiguity, diminish change, and remove struggle from everyday life. The comfortable Christian will continue to fill many church pews for generations to come.

Still others will not want to take the challenge of liberation in their personal Christian way because it will demand full, complete surrender of self into the unknown power of God. To be different, to stand alone or with the minority is too damaging to self-image, to acceptance. Most of all it will be too risky to become "religious" in a complete, albeit balanced, way.

But the task of the liberated Christian is to reach out in love to all of God's children, those who understand and those who do not; those who criticize and those who help; those who need to be comfortable as well as those who are willing to risk.

To risk liberation in Christ is to risk ultimate responsibility, call, challenge, to risk a complete leap of faith, to become one with God and with all of God's children. And in the spirit of that liberation only you can decide how far into freedom you will step. The question is yours to answer:

Will you dare to be a liberated Christian?